AF583306

The Medici and the Etruscans

Research and celebration in the Renaissance

Press & Archeos

Press & Archeos
via Cittadella, 9
50144 Florence
www.pressandarcheos.com
info@pressandarcheos.com

First edition in English language, April 2024
On-demand edition - first update

Iconographic research by the author.
For other photos and illustrations, the publisher has taken care of the relevant permissions from the rights holders. In the case of those whose names were found to be unavailable, we remain at disposal to settle any claims.

The works and models they had created were still too strong and ubiquitous: the roots they had planted in the lands of Italy, especially in Tuscany, were too deep and too widespread for them not to continue to produce new shoots for a long time to come ...

Werner Keller

Introduction

The illustrious members of the Medici family, masters of Florence for no less than three centuries and bearers of its glorious destiny, certainly had the temperament and the ambition to become absolute masters of what had been known since antiquity as Etruria[1].

Hailing from the peasant world of the Mugello, perhaps charcoal burners from Campiano[2] ceramists or healers, when they arrived in Florence they succeeded in time in elevating themselves to the dignity of sovereign princes. This rise was due to their remarkable strategic ability, their capacity for action, their versatile and often grandiose intellect. In addition to political administration and diplomacy, the Medici were involved in religion, the sciences, the arts, letters and military organisation.

And it was precisely during the Renaissance that the Medici, in order to consolidate the myth of their family, reflected the ancient Etruscans, a people already distinguished in archaic times for their political vision and homogeneity of culture, and who in the later centuries BC, renewed by contamination with Hellenistic traditions, were the educators of Rome and Italy.

The Etruscan civilisation took shape and coherence in the 8th century BC and held a dominant position in the whole of Italy at least until the 5th century BC. From the territory between the Arno and the Tiber, the ancient people of Tuscany, heterogeneous and cosmopolitan but already recognisable in their customs and in

1 Roman name to designate the VII Region, established with the Augustan territorial reorganisation, corresponding to the area between the Tiber and Arno rivers, inhabited by the Etruscans. By Diocletian, Etruria (or Tuscia in the late empire) was united with Umbria, forming with it a single region, Tuscia et Umbria, with a governor (corrector) based in Florence (Florentia). In later times it was divided into Tuscia annonaria in the north (united with Emila) and in the south. In the Middle Ages the name Tuscania prevailed. In the organisation of the Catholic Church, Etruria became one of the 18 ecclesiastical regions of Italy. It geographically comprised Tuscany and Tuscan Romagna, with four archdioceses (Florence, Pisa, Lucca and Siena). When Cosimo was elected and the crown of Duke of Florence could not cover the whole of Tuscany, Pope Pius V, with his characteristic energy, decided that Cosimo would be called Magnus Etruria Dux. The name Etruria was resurrected by Napoleon in 1801 for the kingdom created for Louis I of Bourbon, which in 1807 was united with the French Empire by the Treaty of Fontainebleau.

2 A small village near the plain Cafaggiolo where the Medici had one of their most important villas.

the name Rasna/Rasenna (or *Thyrsenoi* for the Greeks), expanded politically and commercially in every direction: in Cisalpine Gaul, with a new dodecapolis[3]; in Roman territory, under the rule of the Tarquins; in Campania, with new emporiums and another dodecapolis. The Etruscans also fought with the Greeks and Phoenicians over the Tyrrhenian Sea, conquering Elba and part of Corsica. After the fall of Veio (396 B.C.), the Roman expansion reduced them to the borders of Tuscany and upper Lazio, with part of Umbria, between the mouths of the Arno and Tiber rivers, where they had already formed a confederation of twelve cities ruled by Lucumoni. During the 4th century the Etruscan cities fell one by one under the rule of Rome. It was not until 90 B.C. that the Tuscans obtained the right to full Roman citizenship, i.e. the recognition that they belonged to the culture to which they had contributed so much, influencing it in religion, art and architecture.

The Rasna people must be seen as the product of events that took place on the Italian peninsula. Despite their openness to Hellenism and the legends that linked them to Anatolia, the Etruscans were jealous of the Italian territory and were the first to express the intention to unite it politically. Perhaps the foundation of Rome itself can be interpreted as a natural development of this intention: the imposition of an Italic-Tuscan factor that, in order to expand, had to shift its centre of gravity further south, incorporating other cultural forms.

The existence of this factor was already perceived in the Renaissance. In the ancient inhabitants of Tuscany we can see the first people capable of adopting an existentially conscious and ambitious outlook, of developing trade, agriculture and pastoralism, and of working metals to perfection. In the tomb paintings, statues and bas-reliefs, one could see a rough realism, sometimes grim, sometimes almost contemptuous, fixed in that

3 According to the Latin literary tradition, the Etruscans already founded a federation of twelve cities in the centre of Italy.

archaic smile full of profound expression: a stylisation already reminiscent of Egypt. In fact, the Etruscan religion found its full expression, as was generally the case in the archaic East, in the cult of the dead and in complex mystery traditions. This "mysterious talent" seemed familiar to the Florentine scholars and thus to the Medici who, from the 15th century onwards, reaffirmed their desire for emancipation from the same Romanism to which their ancestors had directly contributed.

In order to increase their power and possessions, the Florentine dukes and merchants, with their extraordinary financial resources, had the idea of developing the ideal link between the ancient Etruscan monarchies and their new principality. Even before Cosimo I became Duke of Florence in 1537, the greatest writers of the time began to evoke and reinterpret the Etruscan past, some of it rediscovered, some of it imagined. Leonardo Bruni, Giambattista Gelli, Pierfrancesco Giambullari, Leonardo Salviati, Bernardo Segni, Benedetto Varchi, Pier Vettori and many others identified and directed the feelings of the Florentines in their search for historical legitimacy to the political needs of their time, characterised by attempts to unify a Greater Etruria. Sensitive to this intellectual ferment were the artists, who found in the first great archaeological discoveries (monumental tombs, vases, urns and splendid statues) new and highly inspiring ideas for new creations. And it was precisely from the Tuscany of the Medici, fertile with genius and brilliance, that the great intellectual and artistic ideas were born in the "Etruscan Renaissance", which made Western civilisation shine.

Even if the story of this "revival" cannot but be linked to the history of the Medici, further research leads us to believe that the energy of this renaissance is part of the baggage of the Tuscans, and therefore of the relationship between them and their territory. That here, in a land kissed by the climate and courted by beauty, it has always been possible to manifest forms of genius.

Beyond these impressions, however, ours is above all a summary of the studies and consequent artistic gestures that brought the "Etruscan element", with its evidence as well as its mysteries, back into vogue from the 13th century and throughout the Renaissance. The main point of departure and reference remains the in-depth studies of the recent past, in particular those of Giovanni Cipriani[4] in addition to the presentation of some unpublished elements and many curiosities. Therefore, by summarising and recounting those historical moments, also in a popular way, we will pave the way for some in-depth studies in which we have tried to adopt new perspectives on the subject.

In this way, we hope to contribute to the popularisation of a subject that, in our opinion, is still not as well known as it should be.

4 Giovanni Cipriani, *Il mito etrusco nel Rinascimento*, Olschki, Firenze 1980.

The Medici and the Etruscans

The drawing of the Etruscan nation

Between linguistics and mythology: research and celebration

Since Roman times, scholars have looked with curiosity at the Etruscans, their sacred customs and the power they conquered in the not so distant past. The Emperor Claudius, a lover of all ancient things, turned his attention to the origins of Roman civilisation, favoured by his first wife Urgulanilla, who was of noble Etruscan descent. Claudius may have been able to access the archives of the great surviving Etruscan families and obtain important information. Indeed, we know that it was customary for Etruscan nobles to keep a record of their family history and an up-to-date family tree.[5]

Unfortunately, Claudius' books, the *Tyrrhenika* and others, have been lost. They summarised Etruscan history, traditions and, above all, grammar - a truly irreparable loss. In this way, the interest of the cultural world in the Etruscans was shrouded in a thick blanket of mystery that would cover all subsequent centuries.

Except for the fragmentary evidence of the writers of late Latinity, the Etruscans disappeared from view throughout the Middle Ages, removed or simply forgotten, while the classical texts were read only as a function of religious confirmation and in a moralistic key.

Thus, even when some evidence of Etruscan culture was found, everything was done to exorcise it as a trace of a pagan substratum that the evangelisers and the bishops were totally opposed to. Grave desecrators stole valuables such as jewellery and other metal artefacts. In front of the tomb paintings, annoyed by their richness and the serenity of the images, which were incompatible with the sad Middle Ages, they disfigured or blinded the figures depicted (especially the mythological figures with zoomorphic features and therefore obviously satanic).

---

5 This can be deduced from Aulus Persius Flaccus, *Satire*, III,27.

The desire to assimilate the historical and artistic values of the ancient world, and therefore of the Etruscan civilisation, is a merit that should be attributed to the Humanist and Renaissance periods.

The definitive affirmation of the urban dimension as a model for the development of society allowed for the birth and spread of a new figure, that of the man of letters. From the thirteenth century onwards, the bourgeoisie began to play a decisive role in society, slowly at first, then more and more rapidly. The widening of its base and the diversification of its interests favoured and necessitated access to knowledge that had hitherto been guarded only by the Church.

The reintegration of the Etruscans, apart from being understandably fanciful and often unreliable, was not always so much disinterested as directed towards the search for information and concepts, works and images useful for the social, political and spiritual affirmation of the ruling class and its most illustrious representatives. Even before scholars began to study the pre-Roman peoples, the gaze had already turned to the past in order to give the present a historical guise. This was one of the hidden aims of a Florentine institution such as the Accademia Neoplatonica, which Cosimo the Elder wanted to translate and reinterpret treatises from Greece and Constantinople. The thought of the great philosophers was juxtaposed with the post-medieval Christian sentiment and the political-religious needs of the time. One thinks in particular of the work of Marsilius Ficino, which made it possible to establish a continuity with Plato, Plotinus, Augustine, Boethius and others.

At the same time, as early as the 14th century, many scholars devoted themselves to the study of manuscripts and artefacts in order to clarify the existence of the peoples who had first ruled Italy and the role their heritage could play in the geopolitical present.

Thus, animated by a modern spirituality, the reading of the

ancients (Titus Livius, Herodotus, Varro and others) and the poetic inspiration that characterized the culture of the 14th century, scholars began to magnify the ancient Etruscans and speculate on their existence.

As early as the end of the thirteenth century, with Ricordano Malispini's *Historia*[6] the "invention" of the mythical origins of the city of Fiesole can be traced, taken up in the fourteenth century by Giovanni Villani in his Cronica[7] and by Dante in the *Commedia.*[8] Although there is still no mention of Etruscans the foundation is traced back to a pre-Roman world through the mysterious character of Attalante, son of Atlas of Mauritania and father of Dardanus the founder of Troy. Following the Flood, Attalante, on the advice of Apollonius, is said to have founded the first city of Europe (Fia sola) in the Fiesole hills. The legend, also witnessed by Giovanni Boccaccio in the *Genealogy of the Gods*[9] and later by Niccolò Mancini[10] and others, will enjoy wide resonance, becoming the starting point for the narrative inventions of Boccaccio's Ninfale fiesolano. It is important to note the first appearance of the post-diluvian fantasy that will involve hypotheses about the near-eastern origins of the Etruscans for a long time.

Already Villani's *Cronica* takes its start from Bible stories in an attempt, typical of that era, to combine Christian tradition and pagan mythology. It begins with the Tower of Babel and goes back to Noah and his descendants, one of whom was Attalante. Among his sons, Italo was king of a large part of the Italian peninsula, Dardanus founded Troy and Sicanus was the first to settle in Sicily, where he established his kingdom. Through the vicissitudes of the

6 The *Historia antica di Ricordano Malespini gentil'huomo fiorentino. Dall'edificazione di Fiorenza per insino all'anno MCCLXXXI* was written until 1281 and then by his nephew Giacotto until 1286. See Malispini, Storia fiorentina, Multigrafica, Rome 1976, pp. 1 ff.

7 Giovanni Villani, *Nuova cronica*, edited by Giuseppe Porta, vol. I.II.III, Fondazione Pietro Bembo/Ugo Guanda, Parma 2007, vol. I, lib. I, pp. 10-13.

8 Dante Alighieri, *Paradiso*, XV, 119-126.

9 *De Genealogiis deorum gentilium*, written between 1350 and 1368.

10 Niccolò Mancini, *Orazioni o discorsi istorici sopra l'antica città di Fiesole*, Firenze 1729.

Trojan lineage, we come to Aeneas and his landing in Latium, then to the foundation of Rome, the monarchical age and the birth of the Republic with the overthrow of Tarquinus the Proud, until the clash between Rome and Fiesole and the destruction of the latter at the time of the Catiline conspiracy.

In Book II, Villani also provides brief notes on some of the most important Tuscan cities.[11] He never mentions the Etruscans, but when he refers to Chiusi, Cortona and Volterra, he claims that they were built by the first inhabitants of Italy, while of Luni and Pisa he tells us that they already existed at the time of the Trojan War. He also mentions the existence of Populonia, Soana, Talamone and Grosseto, which also took part in the Homeric conflict.

It is obvious that the knowledge about the Etruscans was scarce and unreliable until then, as well as the precise references taken from Latin authors. But it is already possible to feel the trace of a deeper past, perhaps a layer of consciousness that has not yet reached full awareness.

Leonardo Bruni and the beginnings of Etruscan rhetoric

Towards the end of the fifteenth century, the possibility of recovering purely Tuscan antiquities, and thus the memory of the Tyrrhenian, Tuscan or Etruscan peoples mentioned in the sources, seemed to spread slowly among the scholars of Tuscany. As early as the *Invectiva in Antonium Luschum*, written by Coluccio Salutati in response to an anti-Florentine invective by the Visconti in 1403, the legitimacy of the Florentines' expansion was stressed, who, as Etruscans, were to be regarded as the standard-bearers of the libertas Italiae.[12]

---

11 Giovanni Villani "Nuova Cronica", cit., lib. II, pp. 76-82.

12 Eugenio Garin, *Prosatori Latini del Quattrocento* in *La Letteratura Italiana. Storia e Testi*, Ricciardi, Napoli-Milano 1952, vol. 13, pp. 3-37.

The hills of Fiesole where, according to legend, Attalante and his wife Electra arrived (view from San Domenico).

It would be Leonardo Bruni (1370-1444), a great scholar and important supporter of the republican faculties, who would include in the same vast speculation the mythical origins of Fiesole and Arezzo (his native town) with the world of the Etruscans. In his *Historiarum fiorentini populi* (begun in 1414) we find historical information alternating with reflections on traditions and politics. For example, the Lydian origins of the ancient Tuscans, deduced from Herodotus, but also the republican features of their polis, deduced from the reading of Livy, are clarified.

In particular, Bruni notes that each Etruscan community had its own lucumone,[13] just as the free Italian cities had a magistrate and independent governments. Tuscany thus appears as the cradle of the republican order, and Florence in particular, founded by free Roman citizens (Silla's milites) in a traditionally Etruscan land. Florentine expansionism is thus justified as the recovery of former Etruscan territories and suggests a primacy of the Etruscans over

13 *Leonardo Bruni Historiarum fiorentini populi libri XII*, Sumptibus Lazari Zetzneri, 1610, p. 3.

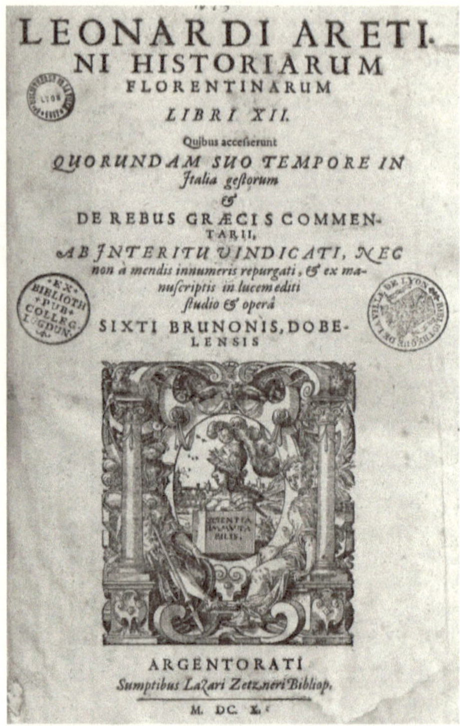
LEONARDI ARETI-
NI HISTORIARUM
FLORENTINARUM
LIBRI XII.
Quibus accesserunt
QUORUNDAM SUO TEMPORE IN
Italia gestorum
&
DE REBUS GRÆCIS COMMEN-
TARII,
AB INTERITU VINDICATI, NEC
non à mendis innumeris repurgati, & ex ma-
nuscriptis in lucem editi
studio & opera
SIXTI BRUNONIS, DOBE-
LENSIS
ARGENTORATI
Sumptibus Lazari Zetzneri Bibliop.
M. DC. X.

Title page of a well-known 1610 edition of Leonardo Bruni's Florentine Stories.

the culture and religion of Rome, which would have drawn its traditions from the Etruscans themselves.

Still far from Etruscology, but strong in a lucidity that would often be "suspended" in the future, Bruni's words are emblematic of a tendency to celebrate the Florentines by referring to the ancient Tyrrhenians. They inaugurate a custom destined to be widely affirmed. Gathering together and giving form to an already widespread sentiment, Leonardo Bruni laid the foundations for a political use of the Etruscan reference, offering it definitively to the men of the Florentine ruling class.

For example, in a work that followed shortly afterwards, Giovanni Gherardi da Prato's Paradiso, the glorification of the splendour and wisdom of the ancient "people of the Tagetes" is taken up again; a parallelism is even drawn between ancient pagan rites and the Christian mass, since in both cases incense would have been used in Tuscany.[14]

In this climate of initial but intense rediscovery, many tried to hoard the Etruscan antiquities that were found here and there in the Tuscan countryside, understanding them as clues or

14 Giovanni Gherardi, *Il Paradiso degli Alberti*, a cura di A. Lanza, Salerno ed., Roma 1975, p. 60, cfr. G. Cipriani, "Il mito etrusco...", cit., pp. 12-13.

tangible proofs of the authority of the Tuscan 'race'. It is difficult to have a clear idea of the scale of the discoveries and trade in these artefacts (or presumed artefacts), but the enthusiasm and immediate interest they aroused is evident, even if the evidence for clear reasons is not much.

Some finds in the tuscan countryside

The most testify about the discoveries comes from the letters between scholars, to confirm an interest to the Etruscans from the best intellectuals of Tuscany, even esoterist. The testimony of the humanist Antonio Ivani (1430-1482), chancellor of Volterra from 1466 at the behest of Piero di Cosimo de' Medici, is interesting. Ivani, who also corresponded with Marsilio Ficino, was a friend of Nicodemo Tranchedini da Pontremoli, Sforza's orator in Florence and his son's tutor. In two letters to Tranchedini, one in 1466 and the other in 1473, he informed him of the discovery in Volterra of two Etruscan tombs, the first of which was just outside the city walls on the road to Pisa.[15]

In the same period, Giorgio Vasari, grandfather of the writer and artist, tells of the discovery in Arezzo, at the time of Bishop Gentile Urbinate, of the remains of ancient kilns and of fragments and whole vases found nearby and donated to Lorenzo the Magnificent. The Medici collection, begun by Cosimo the Elder, grew during the reign of Lorenzo, to whom vases and other artefacts were sent. These included forgeries, such as the terracotta urn given to him by Siena in 1492, engraved with the name of Porsenna and even containing his ashes.[16]

A curious case that testifies to the Medici's interest in Etruscan

15 G. Bartoloni, P. Bocci Pacini, *La divulgazione di scoperte di antichità etrusche a Firenze da Lorenzo a Cosimo*, pp. 373-406, in *Archeologia Classica* vol. 56, L'Herma di Bretschneider, 2005, pp. 373-378 e 393-398.

16 G. Cipriani, "Il mito etrusco nel...", cit., pp. 29-31.

finds is that of a small statue of Venus, 50 centimetres high, currently kept in Villa Corsini, and alluded to in a manuscript of 1505 cited by Anton Francesco Gori.[17] Clearly the work is not of ancient workmanship but according to contemporary historians it was acquired as such by one of the Medici, perhaps Lorenzo or more probably his son Giovanni, the future Pope Leo X. One reason for the interest in the work is the inscription in Etruscan letters on the base, which seems to be inspired by two authentic inscriptions, one on the stele of Avile Tite and the other on the statue of Kourotrophos. Both works were found in Volterra at the end of the 15th century and the inscriptions were reproduced for the first time in Raffaelino Maffei's *Commentari urbani* in 1506.[18]

Among the earliest collectors were undoubtedly the Medici: Cosimo the Elder and Lorenzo acquired and exhibited antiquities, often making them available to the public and to artists for study.

Artists and Etruscan heritage in the Tuscany of the "new Lucumoni"

In the middle of the fifteenth century, Florence was perhaps the most important city in Europe: a financial hegemony that soon brought with it the need for spiritual legitimacy and the consequent search for confirmation in the past. The reference to the world of Republican Etruria was not enough to explain the new political circumstances, and other figures and concepts came to the fore, capable of representing the idea of a lordship over the city. Researchers have focused, for example, on the expansionist and anti-Roman force of Porsenna,[19] proposing the Etruscan

17 Biblioteca Marucelliana di Firenze, MS A198, c 38r.

18 G. Bartoloni, P. Bocci Pacini, "La divulgazione di scoperte...", cit., pp. 379-388.

19 Let us recall the poem by Leonardo Dati (1360-1425) *De Gestis Porsennae Regis Etruscorum Clusinorumque* (written between 1458 and 1460), in which the lucumone's exploits are superimposed on those of "Baccus Piccolomo" (in a celebratory key for the Piccolomini family); Dati claimed to have translated part of the text from a late antique original by Caius Vibenna of Montepulciano. The figure of Porsenna and his story have come down to us from Pliny the Elder,

world as an ideal antecedent to the fifteenth-century situation in which Lorenzo the Magnificent was hailed as Tusciae Dominus, the 'needle of the scales' of Italian and European politics.[20] In this sphere, and especially under Lorenzo's rule, artists played a crucial role, drawing inspiration from the ancient for important new creations.

Monumental tombs, discovered accidentally during agricultural work, attracted the attention of architects and painters, who visited them in order to deduce lost assumptions. It was precisely at this time that several events provided evidence of the Etruscan presence in the Florentine countryside. The right jamb of the tomb of the Mula (in Quinto Fiorentino, nearby Florence) bears the dates 1481 and 1484, indicating that the mound was explored at that time. And it is from this period that *De Re Aedificatoria*[21] was published, in which Leon Battista Alberti, already in the introduction, speaks of "our ancients". Alberti was also inspired by the Etruscans in his architecture, as in the case of Sant'Andrea in Mantua (1460)[22] or the Malatesta Temple in Rimini (1453). In these monuments, the protagonist is the arch (an invention traditionally attributed to the Etruscans, think of the doors of Volterra) inscribed in the modulations of a Tuscan temple.

The Etruscan factor seems to appear here and there in architecture, sculpture and painting, sometimes as a trait d'union that can unite them in a common aesthetic. Donatello had

---

Dionysius of Halicarnassus and others. Porsenna, as king of Etruria (head of the Dodecapolis?), is said to have taken part in an important battle against Rome, allying himself with the exiled king Tarquinius the Proud, at the end of the 6th century BC. Scholars such as Leon Battista Alberti, Antonio Averulino known as Filarete, Michele Capri and others have referred to Porsenna.

20 This is how he is referred to in letters and writings of the time, including Niccolò Valori's (1464-1530) *Laurentii Medicei Vita*, published in Florence in 1568 with the Diario di B. Buonaccorsi.

21 Written at an earlier date, during Alberti's stay in Rome at the court of Nicholas V, around 1450.

22 The layout of the church is inspired by two fundamental concepts: the arch and the temple, already suggested in the façade. The temple is avowedly 'Etruscan', as the architect stated in a private correspondence. Silvia Medde, *Leon Battista Alberti*, in the Encyclomedia, www.oilproject.org.

In the Malatesta Temple in Rimini, also designed by Alberti, we can see 'Tuscan' elements such as the use of the arch, characteristic of Etruscan city gates, and the large base, typical of Etruscan temples, with a continuous Ionic frieze.

already taken up ancient imagery in the throne with sphinx heads of the Madonna of Padua (1450) or in certain dancing putti and ornamental motifs similar to those found in Etruscan paintings and bronzes. Worthy of mention are the tondi in the old sacristy of San Lorenzo with stories of the Evangelists, dating from before 1443. In general, the results obtained with the "stiacciato" technique can be related to the aesthetics of ancient vascular painting. Another interesting example of Donatello's work is the one cited by Raymond Bloch for the image of St. George in Orsanmichele, whose face resembles that of the boy's head known as "di Malavolta". This terracotta from the sanctuary of Portonaccio is on display in the Museum of Villa Giulia (late 5th century BC).[23]

23 Raymond Bloch, *Gli Etruschi*, Il Saggiatore, Milan 1977, p. 169. Discovered only in 1916, Donatello may have seen a similar find, but Bloch speaks first of "similarities in the temperament of the artists". Assigned to the "post-Phidacian circle", the work can be attributed to Greek craftsmen or those influenced by Greek masters (A. M. Moretti Sgubini, *Veio, Cerveteri, Vulci, città etrusche a confronto*, L'Erma di Bretshneider, Rome 2001, p. 74.

Left, one of the "tondi" in the Old Sacristy of San Lorenzo (Florence) in which Donatello depicts St. Mark with the Lion. Above, right, a painting on a Hellenic school vase from Vulci representing Oedipus and the Sphinx, dated 470 B.C. (the image has been mirrored to make the similarities more obvious).

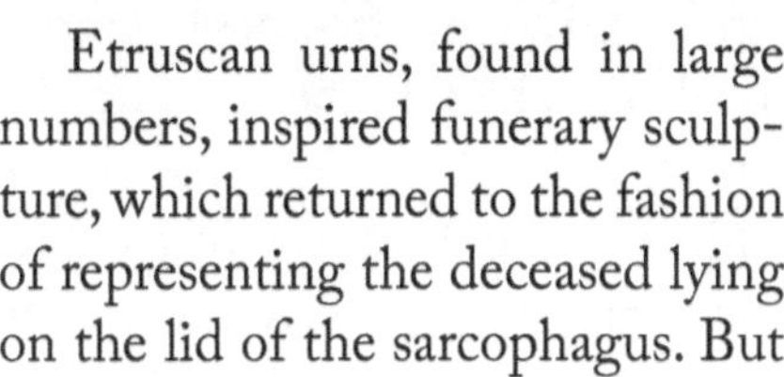

Etruscan urns, found in large numbers, inspired funerary sculpture, which returned to the fashion of representing the deceased lying on the lid of the sarcophagus. But not lying down and lifeless, but facing the visitor with a watchful gaze, the face supported by the arm, the knee raised. Just as the ancient Etruscan lords used to present themselves. Examples of this are the funeral monuments made by Andrea Sansovino (who had trained in Florence) for the Cardinals Ascanio Sforza and Girolamo Basso Della Rovere in Santa Maria del Popolo in Rome (1505-1507).[24] The figure of the pontiff lying awake on his sarcophagus also appears in San Pietro in Vincoli in the Funeral Monument to Julius II, although this solution was not present in Michelangelo's first project (c. 1505).

Returning to Sansovino, we recall the existence of a terracotta statue of Porsenna, Lucumone of Chiusi, commissioned between 1514 and 1520 for the town of Montepulciano.[25] (All that

---

24 For further information see G. Cipriani, "Il mito etrusco...", cit., p. 31, and also Simonetta Valtieri, Il "revival" etrusco nel Rinascimento toscano, in L'Architettura, XVII, 1971, p. 548.

25 Cardinal Antonio da Monte, Sansovino's protector, was also archpriest of Montepulciano, which had recently returned to Medici influence. The head is now in a private collection. M. A.

remains of the statue is the head, with a dour expression worthy of a Medici duke. As we have already seen, supposed "urn" of the same Porsenna was donated by the people of Siena to Lorenzo the Magnificent (or to Leo X)[26]: undoubtedly one of the many cases of fake artefacts from that period.

It was precisely the urns and ancient vases collected by the Medici that were studied by the aforementioned artists and others, as can be seen in many "early" works: From Michelangelo's famous Battle of the Centaurs[27] (1492) to an engraving by Pollaiolo, the Battle of the Nudes (1472), in which the bodies facing each other are captured, in the ancient manner, in the fullness of dynamic gesture. They seem to be arranged according to a geometry that we find in Paolo Uccello and later in Vasari's great frescoes). Among the lesser known cases, there is also that of Francesco Martini da Siena (1439-1501), who painted a fighting scene, copying it from a Hellenistic urn from Chiusi.[28] These masses of fighting figures, inspired by subjects sometimes suggested by the literati themselves, can be related to the bas-reliefs found on ancient funerary vessels.

In Pollaiolo's mature works, the influence of Etruscan vase and mural painting is evident. For example, in a fresco found in the Villa della Gallina (Arcetri, Florence), where agile dancing figures and dionysian images appear. It is difficult to say whether in this case, as in others, the artists were looking for a reference to Tuscan splendour or to antiquity in general.

Perhaps, as early as Botticelli's Primavera (1478), we can sense

---

Turchetti, Sulle orme di Porsenna, Chiusi, 21 August 2018 (brochure), cf. P. Refice, S. Gatta, G. M. Scarpellini, *Andrea Sansovino, profeta in patria*, Icona, Arezzo 2016.

26 The urn would have been found 'at the time of Alfonso Petrucci Vescovo (...) and offered by his relatives to Leone X'. Girolamo Gigli, *Del Collegio petroniano delle balie latine e del solenne aprimento di questo anno 1719 in Siena*, Francesco Quinza, Siena 1729, p. 41, cf. M. A. Turchetti, "Sulle orme...", cit.

27 For this work, the artist, who was still in his teens, was probably inspired by the ancient sarcophagi in St Mark's Garden. S. Risaliti, F. Vossilla, *Michelangelo. La zuffa de centauri*, Electa, Milan 2008.

28 Giovannangelo Camporeale, *Gli Etruschi*, storia e civiltà, Utet, Torino 2005, p. 17.

Tomb of Julius II in S. Pietro in Vincoli (Rome), detail of the statue of the pontiff lying between the Sybil and the Prophet. It seems that this solution was already included in the fifth project for the completion of the monument (1532) but was only realised in 1542 by Tommaso Boscoli (sixth project).

the sublime development of the models of certain Etruscan funerary paintings, in which the figures are arranged in a sparsely three-dimensional scene and in naturalistic circumstances characterised by flowers, garlands, plants and trees. These elements never impose themselves on the human figures, but accompany the gestures of the characters, which are arranged in sequence or involved in small group actions, such as Zephyrus grasping Chloris.

A "typically" Etruscan narrative structure can be seen in the Medici frescoes that Pontormo would paint many decades later in Poggio a Caiano (1519-1521), depicting the myth of Vertumno (as reinterpreted by Ovid). This mythological figure, the principal Etruscan deity (called Velthune, Velth or Voltumna), would be the protagonist of Arcimboldi's extreme synthesis (1590),[29] the paroxysmal declaration of a "style" that had completed its own great cycle within a century.

Even Leonardo da Vinci is said to have been inspired by a visit

29 See Giovanni Spini, *Vertumno and Arcimboldo*, contained in *addendum* of the first Italian Edition of this book: *Etruschi e Rinascimento*, Press & Archeos, Firenze 2018.

One of the entrances to the Montecalvario tumulus in Castellina in Chianti (province of Siena).

to an Etruscan burial mound discovered during the Renaissance, testifying to the curiosity of artists about what comes out of the ground. In the Cabinet des Dessins of the Louvre, there is a drawing of a project by Leonardo for the construction of a mausoleum (around 1507). Although the drawing has six rather than four hypogeal tombs, it bears a striking resemblance to the large tomb of Montecalvario in Castellina in Chianti, dating from the end of the 7th century BC.[30]

Still on the subject of architecture, works to improve the fortifications of Perugia led to the discovery of a series of Etruscan inscriptions and objects, which were studied by the architect Antonio da Sangallo the Younger (1484-1546) in the early 1440s. Antonio attempted to design a reconstruction of the

30 An important testimony exists in the manuscript collection of Pighius, compiled in the second half of the 16th century, *Reliquiae epigraphòn kaì perigraphòn Romanorum*, coll. St. Vin. Pighius, now in the Staatsbibliothek zu Berlin, including a letter written in Latin and sent from Florence on 10 February 1507. The document contains the report of the discovery of an Etruscan tomb found near Castellina, describing the opening of the burial chamber and its plan, in the shape of a cross with a cell at the bottom and side chambers along the corridor, as can also be seen in the corresponding graphic reproduction, which clearly inspired Leonardo da Vinci's drawing now in the Louvre.

Mausoleum of Porsenna according to Varro's description, handed down by Pliny[31] and already taken up by Alberti. When he was commissioned by Pope Paul III to build the fortress of Perugia, he reproduced the Porta Marzia in some drawings, again inspired by ancient examples, with the intention of placing it in its original position.[32]

The Tuscan architecture of Lorenzo and his successors was thus inspired by the Vitruvian Tuscanic order,[33] which characterises the most beautiful buildings in the city, where the ashlar ("bugnato") ornamental motif returns with the Boboli stone, 'grey and Etruscan', contrasting with the white Roman marble. The prototype of this style is Palazzo Medici-Riccardi, whose design was commissioned by Cosimo il Vecchio to Michelozzo, who demanded sobriety and grandeur.

In Florence, in little more than a century, the rediscovery of learning and the aesthetic renaissance had come together in an ideal synthesis, the cradle of the future speculation.

The Etruscan epic of Annio da Viterbo

From a historiographical point of view, the event that most marked a turning point in the perception of "Etruscan greatness" is probably not the work of a Florentine, but of a scholar from the city of Viterbo (Lazio). Victim of the "Etruscan charm", or a clever master of its exploitation, he was able to imagine and reinterpret an Etruscan myth of great symbolic power, linking it to the origins of the "true faith". He also offered an apparatus of references of considerable usefulness for Tuscan rhetoric. We are

31 *Nat. Hist.*, XXXVI,19.

32 Sangallo had the door dismantled and moved four metres away from its original position, integrating it into the outer walls of the Rocca Paolina.

33 The great architect Vitruvius Pollone in his *De Architectura* (1st century A.D.) dictates the rules for the construction of public buildings, private houses and sacred buildings in the Tuscanic or Etruscan style.

Facies tūc agri hui⁹ istar arcus erat: cui⁹ corda esset alue⁹ Thyberis. Cornua ad solis quidē ortū rupes Auētina & ad occasū capitolina: media palatina. Eadē palatina rupes thyberim a frōte prospicit: a sinistris Celio: a dextris Exquilino iungitur. Auentinus item a fronte Thyberim & Capenā tenet: ad dextra Celiolo ac Viminali heret.

Vides itaqz thyberi ueluti cordā arcus. Cernis septē rupes q̄s antiquoqz alii mōtes alii colles uocauerūt. Aspicis eos istar arcus sesi sibi mutuo succedere. Cornua uides duo: ab occasu qdē rupē Tarpeiā siue Capitoliū: ubi pricipio fuit Saturnia: & a q̄ late Saturnia dicta ē terra: ut ait Varro in prio de ligua latina ab ortu uero solis Auentinā rupē: ubi Ital⁹ Capenā cōdidit a q̄ primū porta Capena: que postea Hostiēsis: qa ad urbē ducit Hostiam: nūc sancti Pauli dicit: quia ducit ad eī⁹ sacrū locū

A page from an Annian manuscript (late 15th century).

talking about the Dominican theologian Giovanni Nanni, alias Annio da Viterbo (1432-1502) - also known as Joannes Annius Viterbiensis. He was an extroverted Dominican friar, motivated by a desire to gain the approval of secular authorities (he was held in high esteem by Pope Alexander VI), and already distinguished as a preacher as well as a connoisseur of oriental languages. Annio published the 17-volume *Antiquitatum variarum* in 1498.[34]

With the help of epigraphic and archaeological documents, often fanciful and false (such as the work of Mirsilo of Lesbos: De origine Italiae et Turrenorum), the scholar linked the Etruscan record directly to biblical history. He wanted to prove that the Etruscans were descended from Noah (identified with Vertumno),

34 *Antiquitatum variarum volumina XVII* is the abbreviated name by which the work published at the end of the 15th century under the original title of *Commentaria fr. Ioannis Annii Viterbiensis super opera diversorum auctorum de antiquitatibus loquentium*, Roma, Eucharius Silber, 1498.

that their language was Semitic, that their left-handed writing was reminiscent of Hebrew, and that they had civilised Italy long before the Greeks and Romans.

In Annio's work, the ancient people of Tuscany are elevated to the level of myth: the classical world, the Old Testament and medieval legends intersect, emphasising the universal dimension of human history. The Etruscans were one of the first peoples to populate the world after the Great Flood, and Noah himself had led them to distant Kitim, "quam nunc Italiam nominant". The Patriarch would have taught the Tuscans every branch of knowledge, including religious practices.

With Annio's writings, the authority of the ancient Etruscan people regained its lost positions, asserting an original superiority, even over Rome. The author seems almost to be the first spokesman of the Medici in the enterprise of asserting their power: the Etruscan government was not free and democratic, but in the hands of a duce, as the figure of Porsenna (the mythical king of Chiusi) would demonstrate. The Lucumonians with their priestly, judicial and political functions, once exalted as republican magistrates, became, in the writings of Annio, petty sovereigns, vassals of a single powerful monarch. And there is no place for the *poleis*, but everything falls into an oligarchic and conservative structure: "Hoc nomen Larthes". The republican tendency that had inspired Leonardo Bruni, Coluccio Salutati and others at the beginning of the 15th century is absent here, due to the different historical moment and probably also to the proximity of Rome and its power.

Annio's skill lies in his ability to captivate the reader, telling a complex and believable human story[35] albeit one based on inventions and false discoveries. For example, an "Osirian marble" that would link Viterbo to Osiris, or a slab/table of King Larth

35 For more information, see Riccardo Fubini, *Annio da Viterbo nella tradizione erudita toscana* in *Storiografia dell'Umanesimo in Italia da Leonardo Bruni ad Annio da Viterbo*, in Storia e Letteratura, Roma 2004.

of Breton resemblance; as well as a multitude of epigraphs with acronyms of arbitrary interpretation...

The work was even translated into the vernacular, and centuries passed before its incoehrence was demonstraeted, although there is no doubt that the spark that sprang from this writer's inventions stimulated research destined for a different kind of scientific glory.

From Florence to Rome: Canisius and Leo X

The interest in Tuscan antiquities, already well established in Florence, spread to papal Rome with the election in 1513 of Pope Leo X alias Giovanni, son of Lorenzo de' Medici

For the new Pope, it was particularly important that the ancient Tuscans should be as closely associated with the Romans as possible, and that they should be anything but obscure, so that he could establish links that would be immediately useful for his propaganda. In this vision, Giovanni de' Medici found a valuable ally in the cardinal and general of the Augustinians, a fellow-citizen of the eccentric Annio: Egidio Antonini Canisio da Viterbo (1469- 1532).

In Florence, Canisio met Marsilio Ficino, whose student and friend he was, and with whom he perfected the study of Neoplatonic doctrines and their compatibility with Christianity. In the spring of 1497, Cardinal Riario, protector of the Augustinians, who held the Viterbo man in high esteem, called him back to Rome, where he obtained his doctorate in theology. An extraordinarily effective orator, compared by some to Demosthenes, he was in contact with the leading Roman intellectuals and soon became a Cardinal of the Holy See.

From the point of view of historical reconstruction, Canisius represents in some respects a synthesis between the fantastic needs (represented by Annio) and Florentine Neoplatonism. In the *Historia viginti saeculorum*, the scholar reconstructs the Etruscans as coming from Chaldea (Mesopotamia). Thus, Etruscan history would have a parallel development with Jewish history and the twelve Lucumoni of Etruria would correspond to the patriarchs of the tribes of Israel. Janus, an ancient pre-Roman deity, could be identified with Noah. The Etruscans would therefore be the chosen people of Italy, where they arrived with the aim of colonising it.

Canisius argued that the sacred was inseparable from every aspect of Etruscan life. Again, just as twelve were the cities they founded in the new land, twelve were the apostles, in a forerunner of Christian holiness. If Leo X may have been interested in highlighting the links between the Etruscans/Tuscans and the Romans, Canisius' celebratory intentions went much further. It was the Etruscans who had already shown to the other peoples the reasons of God, the only Creator of the Universe, foreshadowing with their prophecies the events of the following centuries and the affirmation of the new redeeming law, almost as if they were the first missionaries of history!

Canisius, who attributed the etymology of Tyrrhenus to a derivation from turris (an intuition of his compatriot Annio), even proposed the erection of a very high monument in Rome to celebrate the Etruscans as champions of faith and sanctity. It would seem, then, that in dealing with these remote inhabitants of Latium and Tuscany, who were still understood in a vague and mysterious way, scholars were seized by an inspiration that gave rise to astonishing hypotheses. It is almost as if the fascination of archaeological images were a kind of magic.

Cosimo I and the project of a Tuscan nation

After the siege of 1530, the abolition of the Republic and the brief duchy of Alessandro de' Medici,[36] Florentine politics were

36 After the fall of the Florentine Republic, Charles V and Pope Clement VII wanted Alessandro dei Medici, believed to be the son of Lorenzo II, to rule Florence with the title of Duke. Alessandro was murdered in 1537 by an assassin of Lorenzino de' Medici, known as Lorenzaccio,

taken over by Duke Cosimo I, a decisive figure in the search for common ground between Tuscany and ancient Etruria. After becoming Grand Duke of Tuscany in 1569,[37] Cosimo sought to qualify himself as Magnus Dux Etruriae, emphasising his affiliation with an alternative cultural tradition to Rome and implying expansionist aims. Indeed, ancient Etruria was notoriously larger than sixteenth-century Tuscany.

Cosimo left his residence in Via Larga for the Palazzo Vecchio, demonstrating his desire for absolute dominance. He therefore sought in the cultural and literary life of Tuscany elements that would continue the consolidation of his hegemony, also in an ideological sense. He saw in the written and spoken language a precious tool for political propaganda, the elimination of territorial divisions and particularisms, a common script to speed up the administrative bureaucracy.

For this reason, Cosimo gave legal status to the Accademia degli Umidi, creating the Accademia Fiorentina, in 1541. The Umidi ("wet men")[38] were a group of men of letters who had already gathered in the house of Giovanni Mazzuoli, known as Padre Stradino, with the aim of extending the Tuscan language. The study of the Etruscans found ample space in this environment.

The cultural organisation of the Accademia marked the triumph of the Medici cultural policy. The Duke was able to bind the most diverse artistic and literary manifestations to himself and to his will, and thus to direct them personally. The most important literary figures of the time became members of the Accademia,

---

who was then forced to flee. Finding no family worthy of the title, Cosimo, son of Giovanni delle Bande Nere and Maria Salviati, a descendant of Cosimo the Elder's brother (Lorenzo, also known as the Elder), was reluctantly chosen. The young man, who until then had lived in Mugello, proved to be more enterprising than expected and soon took control of the Council of Five Hundred.

37 In that year, at the behest of Pope Pius V, the Duchy of Florence was elevated to the status of Grand Duchy of Tuscany with the bull of 27 August 1569, 'the draft of which was the result of close collaboration between Torelli, one of Cosimo's secretaries, and the lawyer Nofri Camaiani, president of the Papal Letters'. Marcello Verga, *Dicembre 1569: la concessione del titolo granducale ai Medici in Portale Storia di Firenze*, December 2012, http://www.storiadifirenze.org/.

38 In connection with this curious definition, the components had equally metaphorical names, all related to water: "limpido", "scrosciante", "zampillo", etc. (clear, roaring, gushing, ...)

Equestrian statue of Cosimo I de' Medici in Piazza della Signoria in Florence (1587-1594) by Giambologna.

which was linked to the Studio Fiorentino,[39] so that the offices of rector of the Studio and consul of the Accademia were held by the same person. Politics and culture were to go hand in hand, and it was agreed that the Consul would sit on the Council of the Ducato. Cosimo renewed the splendour of the past with his court and, determined to demonstrate the continuity of his family's patronage, he protected artists, purchased Etruscan-Roman antiquities and promoted any activity that could enhance his prestige.

Santi Marmocchini or Marmocchino (c. 1470 - 1548), a

39 This was the Studium Generale, recognised as a university by Clement VI in 1348 but already in existence in 1321, later confirmed as an imperial university (1364) and linked to the University of Pisa, where Lorenzo the Magnificent wanted it to be based.

Dominican from San Casciano val di Pesa,[40] was one of the first faithful spokesmen for this renewed interest in ancient Tuscany. His *Dialogo in defensione della lingua toschana*, written between 1541 and 1545 and dedicated to Cosimo I, not only dealt with the linguistic disputes of the Florentine Academy, but was also notable for the new archaeological methods it employed. In order to prove the origin of the Tuscan language from the Hebrew via the Etruscan, the monuments and artefacts that were constantly coming to light were analysed in detail.

At the end of the Dialogo, the language proposed by Marmocchini is refuted by an alphabetical list of Hebrew etymata, from which as many Tuscan terms would derive, sealing the claim of a direct Hebrew origin. The suggestive hypotheses of Annio and Canisius were thus taken up again with the intention of a specific refutation, without renouncing the link with Old Testament antiquity, which seems to be the winning aspect of these theories.

Pietro Bembo and the 'vulgar language'

The Florentine language was "awakened from its slumber" at the beginning of the sixteenth century by the studies of Cardinal Pietro Bembo (1470-1547), considered by the contemporary cultural world to be "the greatest man Italy had at that time".[41] As a child, he followed his father, a senator of the Venetian Republic, to Florence, where he met the great Lorenzo and learned to appreciate the Tuscan language, which he would later prefer to that of his native city.

It was Pietro Bembo who found the winning solution to the problem of the Italian language, that is, to the debate that raged

40 We know that he took the Dominican habit in 1491 and that he received his theological and linguistic training during the years of Savonarola's preaching at the College of St Mark. See L. Saracco in the Enciclopedia Treccani cf. Dizionario Biografico degli Italiani, 2008, v. 70.

41 This sentence by Leonardo Salviati is taken from *Orazione in lode della fiorentina favella*, 1564.

at the beginning of the century on the model of linguistic and literary unification. Such a unification could only take place on the basis of literary tradition, because languages spread and become established when there is an awareness of their value and, therefore, recognition by illustrious men. These masters were mainly Florentines and Tuscans.

As a young man, Bembo had witnessed the solemn restoration of Dante's tomb in Ravenna, commissioned by his own father. The event probably left a deep impression on him. The deepening of his knowledge of the masters of the past continued in Rome, where Peter visited the main sites of Christianity and antiquity. After a meeting with Poliziano, his humanistic passion took shape, despite his first political posts, through the writing of poems in Latin and the study of Greek. He perfected his Greek during a stay in Messina. He then lived in Ferrara, in Venice, Padua, Urbino and several times in Rome, alternating his ecclesiastical and diplomatic career with that of a poet. He published works on grammar, history and poetry, as well as editions of the books of Dante and Petrarch, which the publisher Manuzio brought together for the first time with the classics of antiquity.

In 1525 he published the *Prose della 'vulgar lingua'* (written in 1512), a fundamental work in the history of Italian culture, which emphasised the superiority of the Florentine language over all other Italian dialects. However, this was not the language spoken by the people, but rather the language in the forms achieved by Petrarch and Boccaccio, the one the model for poets, the other for prose writers.

Bembo proposed important solutions to the question of the choice between Latin and the vernacular, bringing new elements on the nature of the vernacular itself, its origins and its primates, analysing grammatical and lexical aspects with rigour and refinement. He also proposed a link between the Tuscan and Provençal languages, with particularly explanatory results.

Medal with the profile of Giovan Battista Gelli (16th century). Photo by Sailko, C.C. 3.0.

Gelli and Giambullari: linguistics meets mythology

Among those who, like Ariosto and others, greeted Bembo's prose with interest or enthusiasm was the Florentine scholar Giambattista Gelli (1495-1563), a key figure in the linguistic debate on the Etruscan origins of the Tuscans.

Of humble origins, the son of winegrowers and a shoemaker by trade, at the age of twenty-five, having learnt Latin, he devoted himself to philosophical studies, gaining the sympathy of Florentine scholars and beginning an important literary production. He never ceased to practice his humble trade and to participate in the relevant guild.

Among his most famous works are *I capricci del bottaio* (1546), reasoning between a cooper and his soul (included in the first index of forbidden books[42]) and *La Circe* (1549), a dialogue

42 The *Index librorum prohibitorum* was created by Pope Paul IV in 1559 with the intention of listing certain works that no one should dare "write, publish, print or have printed, sell, buy, lend,

between Odysseus and his companions transformed into animals.

Gelli attended the Accademia Platonica and the Accademia degli Umidi (later the Accademia Fiorentina), strengthening his emblematic image as an artisan-literary. In September 1553, Cosimo I appointed him ordinary reader of the *Commedia* at the Accademia Fiorentina, and from that year until his death he recited nine Dante readings published annually. Gelli's readings had a great influence on Dante's interpreters throughout the Florentine 16th century.

Among Gelli's writings is the *Trattatello sulle origini di Firenze* (Treatise on the origins of Florence), written around 1543 and dedicated to Cosimo I, in which he traces the route of the connection between the Chaldeans/Arameans and the Florentines. The influence of Annio's *Antiquitatum variarum*, whose suggestive hypotheses had been circulating for decades through the writings of Canisius and Marmocchini, is evident.

The treatise supports the theory of the foundation of the first post-diluvian civilisation in Tuscany by Noah, identified with Janus, the bearer of a culture that preceded the Greco-Roman one, namely the Etruscan one. The Latin language was thus surpassed in antiquity by the Etruscan language. Even more important, however, was the value placed on the Tuscan language, its analysis and its progress. The updating of these mythological-linguistic theses, despite not a few perplexities (above all, as we shall see, those of Varchi and then Borghini), provided a solid propagandistic basis for the idea of a regional Tuscan state under the aegis of the Medici. We are in fact in the years when Cosimo expanded the Duchy of Florence with the intention of ruling over the whole of Etruria. The 'Aramean thesis' appealed to the Duke and some scholars directed their research in this direction, while the transformation of the Accademia can be read as an authoritarian closure aimed at protecting the work of those who

---

give away, or on any other pretext, receive, keep, keep or have kept...". Among the many works banned were Dante's *De Monarchia* and Boccaccio's *Decameron*.

accepted politically useful theses.

Pierfrancesco Giambullari (1495-1555), the son of a poet who had already been in Lorenzo's circle, developed an Etruscan-Jewish perspective, reinforcing and reworking its contents. First a young secretary to Madonna Alfonsina Orsini, he later enjoyed the favour of the Medici family and then of Leo X. In 1515 he was appointed rector of the church of San Pietro in Careggi and in 1527 he became supernumerary canon of the Basilica of San Lorenzo in Florence. He was keeper and librarian of the Laurentian Library and one of the first initiates of the Accademia degli Umidi, then co-founder of the Accademia Fiorentina, for which he wrote the Lezioni, which included Dante readings given between 1541 and 1548, and reports on the grammar of the vernacular. Together with Giovan Battista Gelli, Carlo Lenzoni and Cosimo Bartoli, Giambullari was one of the most important members of the Academy and one of the most trusted 'Cosimians'.[43]

In Giambullari's writings, the solidarity between his position and that of Gelli is evident, so much so that the scholar entitled one of his most important works *Il Gello* (1546), which deals with the problem of the origins of the Tuscan language. Giambullari took up the general lines of the myth told by Gelli, which exalted classical antiquity in order to trace it back, through the Etruscans, to Aramaic, an older and more original stage consisting of the culture and language of Noah. However, his approach differed from that of his colleague and friend, as well as from that of the French philosopher Guillaume Postel (1510-1581), with whom Pierfrancesco corresponded.

In De Etruriae regionis originibus institutis religione et moribus, Postel supported the Aramaean theory in an anti-Roman form and extended it to Gallic origins. The book was published in

43 He drafted for Cosimo the Apparato et feste per le nozze dell'illustrissimo signor duca di Firenze e della duchessa sua consorte, which is a description of the apparatus made for the wedding of Cosimo I with Eleonora di Toledo in 1539. The inscriptions, and therefore the "slogans" on display, were mainly written by Gelli and focus on the Etruscan national discourse, the Duke's closeness to the Emperor and the union of the Tuscan cities under Florentine command.

IL GELLO DI
M·PIERFRANCESCO
GIAMBVLLARI ACCADEMICO
FIORENTINO.
IN FIORENZA MDXLVI.

Frontispiece of Il Gello by Pierfrancesco Giambullari, edition of 1546.

Florence in 1551 and dedicated to Duke Cosimo. By combining the dynastic claims of the Medici into a single cauldron, Postel projected these civilisations into pre-Classical times. The common descent from Noah linked Rome, Etruria and France in a single chain. Contrary to Postel and Annio, Giambullari maintained a relativist attitude and eventually shifted the focus of the question to linguistics.

The decisive proof of the descent of Tuscan civilisation from Aramaic would consist in the quantity of vernacular words that can be traced back to the same root of Aramaic words. Giambullari endeavours to prove his thesis by means of ample examples. The unveiled etymology of Tuscan place names such as 'Firenze',

Portrait of Pier Francesco Giambullari from an edition of the Lectures (1827).

'Arno', 'Etruria' or 'Marzocco', posing itself as an alternative to the Latin derivation, stands as proof of a historical filiation. The result is more credible than in the case of other authors, although the scholar does not shrink from using literary sources to support the veracity of his intuitions. However, the differences with Postel stood out in the context of a controversy over a text by Athenaeus of Naucratis, discovered in the Laurentian Library, which according to the Frenchman confirmed the thesis of the "annian authors" and the arrival of Noah at the shores of Tuscany.[44]

In 1550 the Accademia Fiorentina decided to devote itself definitively to the study of the vernacular: a commission of 'reformers' was set up, composed of Giambullari, Benedetto Varchi, Carlo Lenzoni, Lionardo Tanci and Francesco Torelli. The starting point for this new research was Giambullari's Regole della lingua fiorentina, later printed by Torelli under the title De la lingua che si parla e si scrive in Firenze (1552). The manuscript was presented in 1548, on the birthday of Francis I (25 March), as a tribute to

44 F. Pignatti in *Dizionario Biografico degli Italiani*, vol. 54, 2000.

the future Duke.

The rules are the first real grammar of the Florentine language. The new text aroused great expectations, since the greatest contributions to linguistics had not come from Tuscans, but from Venetians such as Pietro Bembo and Gian Giorgio Trissino.

Giambullari's approach reflects the tendency towards Medicean cultural expansionism: the grammar is aimed at foreigners and young people who want to speak and write in Florentine. The appeal to the spoken language is ideally derived from that of the cultured classes, but not without opening up to more popular expressions, authorised by usage and sometimes transposed from the written tradition.

Giambullari's academic industriousness made him one of the most uncompromising defenders of the vernacular, whether he was promoting its use in scientific, historical and literary works or asserting its independence from Latin in terms of grammatical rules and historical origins. The orthography we use today, which is much closer to pronunciation than to Latin etymology, was initiated by Giambullari himself.

One of the many contributions to this great debate on the Italian language was the *Dialogo della volgar lingua*, in which the Venetian Giovan Pietro Bolzani (better known as Pierio Valeriano, 1477-1558), discussing the distant origins of Italian, emphasised the common features it shared with Latin, Greek and even Etruscan. The ancient links between Rome and Etruria were once again confirmed, Tuscan culture was the oldest, and not only Rome but also Greece, the cradle of civilisation, had learned fruitful lessons from the Etruscans. In short, the interest in the ancient Etruscans was not an exclusively Tuscan question.

The references to this linguistic-ethruscological bibliography show that the myth of Etruscan origins was now present in the most cultivated minds of Florence, and that it was no longer a "ghost" trying to assert itself, ethereal and sepulchral, on the surface of Latinity. Moreover, during the activity of Bembo,

Gelli, Giambullari and others, Duke Cosimo gained ground in every respect in the affirmation of an Etruscan unity and in the legitimation of the dignity of a new Etruria. The Medici state was in full expansion.

While scholars speculated about the primacy of the Florentine language, the Duke made his first inroads into the Lunigiana with the purchase of the territories of Filattiera (1549) and Corlaga (1551) from the Malaspina, and almost at the same time Piombino fell into Medici hands (1552). Shortly afterwards, in 1554, with the help of Charles V, the victory over the eternal rival Siena was achieved, and in 1558 Castiglion della Pescaia and the island of Giglio were sold by the Piccolomini family to the Medici.

At the same time, archaeological finds multiplied as news of Cosimo's interest in the Etruscans spread throughout the city and the countryside. Both Vasari and Cellini recalled the discovery of the Chimera (1554),[45] while Michelangelo had already made a drawing of a bearded god of the underworld wearing a wolf's skin for a headdress, an image perhaps glimpsed in a newly discovered Etruscan tomb.[46]

The great scholars the Duke wanted in Florence

With a view to his project of a great Etruria and the need to legitimise his authority, Cosimo did his utmost to attract the best men of letters in circulation, and in this he was able to overcome the political differences in the organisation of a government and the differences of opinion among his scholars, whose work was protected by the academic institution.

Pier Vettori (1499-1585), a philologist and humanist, took

45 Giorgio Vasari, *Ragionamenti*, 1588, g. 1, r. 4; g. 2, r. 3; Benvenuto Cellini, *Vita di Sé Medesimo*, Cocchi, 1728, t. II, p. 321.

46 Fritz Weege, *Etruskische malerei*, Halle 1921, p. 84, and later Raymond Bloch, Etruschi, cit., p. 169, referring to a Florentine drawing by the Master, already mentions this. The image would be similar to the one visible in the Tomb of the Orcus in Tarquinia discovered in 1868. The intuition has been taken up on several occasions, for example by Margherita Scarpellini in "Andrea Sansovino, profeta in...", cit.

part in the events of his city in his youth. He was a convinced republican, so much so that after the military and political victory of the Medici, following the memorable siege by Charles V, he preferred to retire to San Casciano in Val di Pesa. In 1538, however, Cosimo succeeded in recapturing him and tying this promising scholar to his triumphal chariot.

The Grand Duke entrusted Vettori with the task of reader in the studio, where he taught for decades, winning the favour of the citizens and the devotion of the students. He was one of the greatest teachers of his time, preserving in his teachings the ideals of the ancient Etruscan heritage. He worked on editions of many classics and dealt with subjects ranging from agriculture to science, from rhetoric to moral philosophy, but his main interest throughout his life remained the study of ancient texts. Of particular note are the *Castigationes*, commentaries on Cicero's Familiar Epistles, and editions of works by Varro, Cato and Aeschylus; Euripides' Electra, the late edition of Sallust's works, Aristotle's political and moral writings, and the *Lives of Iseus and Dinarchus by Dionysius of Halicarnassus*. His definitive masterpiece was the edition of *Aristotle's Poetics*. In 1553 Vettori published the first twenty-five books of his Variarum lectionum, which was expanded by a further thirteen in 1569 and republished in its entirety in 1582.

Among the men of letters who contributed to the greatness of the new Etruria is Bernardo Segni (1504-1558). Born into a family of merchants, he was attracted to literary studies and attended Francesco Verino's lectures in Pisa. Initially he worked as a merchant, but due to financial difficulties he was "forced" to serve the Grand Duchy.

A friend of important men opposed to the Medici regime, Segni championed the idea of an aristocratic republic and, when the political climate in Florence became dangerous for such aspirations, he moved to Venice. He then studied law at the University of Padua. The family's economic collapse prompted

Bernardo to return to Florence and implicitly accept the Medici restoration by working for Duke Alessandro. In 1541, he was Cosimo's ambassador to Ferdinand I of Hapsburg, and from then on he held numerous public offices. He was a man of letters, a philologist, a translator of Sophocles' Oedipus Rex and of various works by Aristotle, but above all he was a historian.

Another important figure was Benedetto Varchi (Florence 1503-1565).

His family came from Montevarchi, but his father, Ser Giovanni, was a Florentine and worked as a procurator for the archbishopric. Benedetto received his humanistic education from Gaspare Mariscotti da Marradi and, at the age of eighteen, moved to Pisa to study law, becoming a procurator and notary. After the death of his father, who had left him a considerable fortune, he devoted himself entirely to letters. He learnt Greek from Pier Vettori and studied Provençal.

A republican, a member of the Strozzi family, he left Florence after the return of the Medici. He lived in exile in Venice, Padua and Bologna. In 1543, having exhausted his fortune, he too settled with Duke Cosimo, who gave him honorary posts and, in 1558, the villa of Topaia above Poggio Secco (in the hamlet of Castello). This building had incorporated an ancient Etruscan tomb, now lost.[47]

Varchi's lectures on Dante Alighieri at the Accademia Fiorentina were famous, but he also wrote sonnets, songs and poems in Latin. He translated Boethius' *De consolatione philosophiae* and Seneca's *De beneficiis*; he studied linguistics, literary criticism, ancient history, aesthetics, philosophy, alchemy and botany. During the reign of Francesco de' Medici, he published an important treatise, *L'Hercolano*, on the relationship between the Florentine language and the Etruscans (we will talk about this later).

Thus, in the middle of the 16th century, with this group of

47 It was probably a tholos tomb, the twin of the nearby Montagnola, which collapsed at the time of Varchi or shortly afterwards.

active scholars at the height of their research, the spirits of the Medici court were preparing for what seemed imminent and necessary: the confirmation of Florence as the capital of the Etruscan territory.

After this statement, the debate on the Etruscan language and its origins, in which Varchi, Giambullari and others were protagonists, slowly turned and took other directions, as we shall see after recounting the most important event in the unification of Tuscany.

Top right, Benedetto Varchi in a print taken from L'Omnibus pittoresco (1840); Next, Pier Vettori, engraving taken from a book by J. J. Boissard (mid 17th century).

The Battle of Scannagallo and the affirmation of 'Greater Etruria'

A ceiling panel in the Salone dei Cinquecento shows Cosimo leaning over a table, studying the conquest of the city of Siena.[48] In his desire to extend his dominions over the whole of Tuscany, he saw Siena as the only city that could prevent the implementation of the Great Etruria project.

At the French court, the Florentine outsiders were well received by Queen Catherine de' Medici, who detested her distant cousin and tried to thwart his plans. Meanwhile, Piero Strozzi, Cosimo's rival, succeeded in obtaining the rank of Marshal of France. Spain, too, was not going to let the Duke of Florence realise his dreams and kept him under constant surveillance with its spies, so that he would not escape from the dependence of Charles V. From his relations with Spain, Cosimo hoped to obtain the principality of Piombino, but he had to endure promises and refusals. He was initially content with the Island of Elba, whose defence he obtained in 1548. Meanwhile, Siena had openly offered itself to the French, waiting for events to unfold and preparing for a possible Florentine attack.

Taking advantage of a favourable moment, when the French were fighting Genoa for possession of Corsica, Cosimo prepared the expedition to Siena on the pretext of helping Spain to weaken France politically.

This phase was full of diplomatic and political subtleties. The French were at first favourably disposed towards Cosimo, so much so that King Henry II proposed a marriage between one of his illegitimate daughters and Francesco de' Medici (who had just turned thirteen), thus strengthening the already strong dynastic

48 In Vasari's work there are allegories of fortitude (with a column), prudence (with a mirror), vigilance (with a lamp), patience and silence, sitting in a corner with his finger on his lips. All summed up in the Latin phrase: Bellum cogitans praevenit.

alliances. Cosimo rejected the proposal but did not break the good relations. Meanwhile, from his study in the Palazzo Vecchio, he sent requests for military aid to Spain, seeing in the political moment the possibility of a military venture against Siena.

The battle

The plan for the expedition came to fruition on 26 January 1554, when a large army set out from the Medici fortress of Poggibonsi. One part of the troops went towards Grosseto, another towards Chiusi through the Val di Chiana; a third, under the command of Gian Giacomo Medici,[49] Marquis of Marignano (nicknamed the Medeghino because of his short stature), made a rapid night march towards Siena by the light of the "rificolone"[50] supported on long poles.

The attack on Siena was made from Porta Camollìa, but after an initial success, the Florentines were repulsed by the Sienese, who drove them back to the sound of arquebuses. The next day the long siege of the city began.

Henry II sent more troops from Marseilles to punish the audacity of the Florentine duke who had dared to attack a city outside his domain. But while crossing the Tyrrhenian Sea, a storm delayed the French fleet.

In July 1554, Piero Strozzi, who had rushed to Siena with the French troops, went outside the walls with his troops to break the Medici encirclement and take the war far from Siena. He then moved on to Arezzo to stock up on provisions and to try to get the city to rise up against Florence. At the same time, Marignano's

49 Gian Giacomo, Marquis of Marignano, a member of an upper Italian Medici family and not related to the Florentine Medici, served in Spain and was general of the league between Emperor Charles V and Pope Clement VII. When his brother Giovanni Angelo became Pope Pius IV, the two Medici of Marignano declared their kinship with Cosimo, although in reality this was not the case: the latter obviously found it most useful not to contradict them.

50 The Rificolona festival is an event linked to Florentine folklore. On the 7th of September the city is filled with coloured lanterns. The origins of the magical Rificolona festival are all Florentine.

Giorgio Vasari, Battle of Marciano in Val di Chiana, Palazzo Vecchio, Salone dei Cinquecento, 1554. Image from Wikipedia.

troops distinguished themselves with dramatic actions of plunder and devastation in the Sienese territory.

Cosimo began to insist that Marignano face the enemy in the open, while Strozzi, moving from conquest to conquest, entered Marciano della Chiana. Here Gian Giacomo Medici arrived with his garrisons. After four days of inconclusive skirmishes, the armies faced each other on the hills surrounding the town, separated by the valley of the then dry Scannagallo stream.

The decisive battle began on the morning of 2 August 1554, a scorching day (it had not rained for forty days) when the fate of the city of Siena was decided. The Medici's artillery was superior to that of Siena and Marignano could count on heavy cavalry, three hundred men and fully armoured horses, which the Sienese, who also had more than a thousand horsemen, did not have. The battle began with the charge of the Medici cavalry.

On the edge of the valley, under the command of Strozzi, Italian, Sienese and French soldiers were lined up for Siena, reinforced by German and Grisons mercenaries, for a total of about fifteen thousand men, including one thousand two hundred horsemen. On the other side, Medeghino's troops were evenly matched, made up mainly of Germans, Spaniards and Italians. The fierce battle lasted only two hours and ended disastrously for the Sienese, partly due to the treachery of a standard bearer. A certain Righetto del Campana had been paid with a large quantity of gold coins and fled, dragging the Franco-Sienese cavalry behind him.

Piero Strozzi tried to resist with his infantry alone, but at the end of the day he was forced to retreat to Lucignano, leaving four thousand dead and a hundred flags on the ground, while the Florentine side suffered only a few hundred casualties.

The Battle of Scannagallo, also known as the Battle of Marciano, was Cosimo I's last dynastic battle before the extinction of the family. His dream of ruling over a large part of Etruria had come true: Cosimo celebrated with festivities and works of art. To commemorate the day, in 1561 he founded the Equestrian Order of *Santo Stefano della Vittoria* and had a chapel built on the site of the battle.

It is interesting to read the chronicles of the time to understand the magnitude of this victory. In the *Diario Fiorentino*, Agostino Lapini recounts how Cosimo received the news of the defeat of the republican rebel army led by Piero Strozzi at the battle of Marciano: "*And on the second day of August, 1554, Thursday at half past ten, three couriers came to Florence with garlands on their heads and olive branches in their hands to bring Cosimo, the second Duke of Florence, the happy news of the defeat of Piero Strozzi. And this victory took place near Marciano, in a place called Scannagallo, and it happened that many Gauls, that is to say Frenchmen, died there*".[51]

Cosimo learned of the victory while standing in front of the Church of Santa Trinita, where he then had the great porphyry column from the Baths of Caracalla erected to commemorate the event, on top of which Tadda's statue of Justice was later placed.

51 Agostino Lapini, *Diario fiorentino dal 252 al 1596*, Sansoni, Firenze 1900, p. 112-113.

While in Oltrarno, in Piazza San Felice, a column was erected, again to commemorate the victorious event, on which the statue of Peace was to be placed.[52]

With regard to the column in Piazza Santa Trinita, there is something more to be said: the lower part of the stylobate would have "dimensions and moulding referable to Etruscan altars", while the capital would correspond to the Tuscan order.[53]

Siena, starving, therefore took the cruelest decision, throwing out of the walls the people who were useless for the war, the old men and the children; not the women, because they were also fighting under the command of two nobles (Piccolomini and Forteguerri) and a commoner (a certain Fausti), throwing stones and boiling water from the city walls.

It seems that the Florentines were far from sympathetic to these expellees, and even less so to the peasants who had tried to bring supplies into the city. Cosimo wrote to his secretary Bartolommeo Concini: "*...we deplore the fact and do not wish to be drawn into such things any longer... Concino, you know me, see that things are done well, if you do not want me to be outraged.*"[54] On the contrary, the besiegers were ruthless with those who tried to bring food within the walls, giving orders to hang two peasants for every ten captured.

And "*whoever is found by chance may be hanged without limit.*"[55] More than one thousand five hundred were thus hanged around the city.

On the 17th of April 1555, the flag fell from the Torre del Mangia and Siena, exhausted, opened its gates. However, while the Florentine troops entered in jubilation, seven hundred Sienese families, under the command of the Gonfaloniere Mario Bandini,

---

52 The statue was never hoisted because of the Grand Duke's death. P. Bargellini, E. Guarnieri, *Le strade di Firenze*, Bonechi, Florence 1977, vol. I, p. 346.

53 Gabriele Morolli, "Vetus Etruria...", cit., tavole LXXVIII e LXXXII, in didascalia.

54 Piero Bargellini, *I Medici*, Bonechi, Firenze 1980, p. 249.

55 Ibidem.

fled and reached Montalcino, which was to be the last seat of the Sienese Republic for four more years.

The official capitulation of Siena took place on 27 April 1555: The French were told to leave the city free, and Cosimo sent a garrison of 2,000 men, including Spaniards and Germans, under the command of the Count Sforza of S. Fiora. The Duke demanded that this garrison be well disciplined and that the Sienese be well treated.[56]

Strategy and policy after the surrender of Siena

The capture of Siena did not bring Cosimo any immediate advantages. It took all his cunning and diplomatic skills not to be deprived of the spoils that Spain, France and the papacy were trying to steal from him.[57] A triple game that Cosimo played skilfully and tenaciously for about two years, negotiating with both and trying to exploit each other's rivalries. The conquest of Siena had cost too much effort and money, his subjects were angry at the taxes he had created for them ... in short, Siena had to be Florentine at all costs.

After the death of Charles V, Cosimo continued his "tug-of-war" with the new ruler, Philip, showing devotion to him but without evincing any awe. There is a letter addressed to the Duke of Ferrara in which a feeling of national pride vibrates. Cosimo writes: "*With these great princes it is necessary to govern in such a way that we consider their aims well, help and warn us, and oppose their unjust aims, because we are not inspired by passion for Spain or France, but only by the universal good of Italy, our homeland*".[58]

---

56 Antonio Ferrini, *Compendio di storia della Toscana*, Sansone Coen, Firenze 1840, p. 133.

57 Especially Pope Paul III Farnese, who had arranged for his nephew Ottavio to become the Emperor's son-in-law by marrying Margarita (widow of Duke Alessandro de' Medici), and did not hide his intentions to convince Charles V so that Florence and its state would pass precisely from Cosimo to Ottavio.

58 Letter written in 1558 to Ercole II d'Este, Duke of Ferrara, Modena and Reggio. Piero Bargellini, *La splendida storia di Firenze*, Vallecchi, Vol. II, p. 369.

Giambologna, Cosimo I enters Siena victorious, bronze relief on the base of the equestrian statue of Cosimo I, Piazza della Signoria, Florence.

In July 1557, an ambassador of the King of Spain placed a ring on Cosimo's finger: "*On the third day of July, Saturday evening at 2 o'clock at night, our Duke Cosimo de Medici, second Duke of the City and Republic of Florence, was invested and made true and perpetual lord and master of the City of Siena, by a warrant of King Philip, King of Spain and son of the Emperor Charles V, called the said warrant the Ficarola. Who by order of the said King Philip put a ring on our Duke's finger. Afterwards he gave a rod into his hand and took off his headgear and put it on the said Duke's head; and made him swear on a letter from King Philip and on the gospel, to observe fully all that he had promised to the said King Philip*"[59] This was the ancient rite of investiture of a feud, repeated in Florence to signify that Cosimo received from the Emperor the mandate and not the possession of Siena. At the time, he had to be satisfied with a partial recognition, obtaining the investiture of feudal vassal from

59 Agostino Lapini, "Diario fiorentino...", cit., p. 118.

Philip II, after convincing him of the need to wrest Siena from the King of France and the Pope of Rome.

In 1557, not long after the capitulation of Siena, Emanuele Filiberto, Duke of Savoy and captain of the Spanish, inflicted a definitive defeat on the French at the Battle of San Quentin. The French, who were also conducting the war in Europe, withdrew some contingents engaged in the Sienese, including one led by Pietro Strozzi, who was to die shortly afterwards during the siege of Thionville. When the news reached Florence again Lapini reported "*... how Signor Piero Strozzi, Grand Marshal of the King of France, had died under the city of Triumville valiantly*". Cosimo I could now breathe. The spectre of Filippo Strozzi, "*still lurking in the Fortezza da Basso*", no longer had avengers.[60]

After the peace treaty of Cateau-Cambrésis in 1559, the Franco-Spanish war came to an end and the garrison of Montalcino also surrendered its independence: Cosimo sent troops commanded by Francesco da Montauto to definitively take over the bastion.

If Montalcino was able to maintain its independence for four years, it was also due to the secret aid of Cosimo, who silently supplied the fortress with provisions so as not to create further discontent in the Sienese, according to his complex expansion plans.

Finally, on 10 August 1559, a mass was sung in San Lorenzo "*for the conquest of Montalcino, Grosseto and other towns and places that had been held by the Franks together with the Sienese: no other celebrations were held, except that the said mass was sung*"[61].

Cosimo was now free to travel to Rome, where, on the death of Paul IV, Pius IV, brother of the Marquis of Marignano, had ascended to the papal throne. What more could one wish for? The new pope Giovanni Angelo de' Medici di Marignano, when he was a cardinal, claimed to be related to Cosimo (but he was not); now it was Cosimo who boasted of being related to him and

60 Ibid., p. 122.

61 Ibid., p. 125.

rightly boasted of his friendship. After the deaths of Francis I of France, Philip V of Spain and Pope Paul IV, the Medici once again became one of the most important families in Italy and Europe. In the fullness of this prestige, on 26 October 1560, Cosimo and his wife Eleonora of Toledo set out for Rome, to cross throught his Sienese feud for the first time.

A large part of the conquered were sincerely sympathetic to Cosimo. Lapini wrote: "*He was met at the entrance by fifty cherubs, all dressed in white, with silk curtains and olive curls in their hands, who showed great joy to the cherubs and all the people: of which the Duke, with great tenderness and weeping, took most of them and kissed them*".[62] Cosimo was now forty-one years old, and the blood of his father (and above all that of his grandmother Caterina Sforza) had perhaps softened in his veins. For his personal insignia he had chosen a turtle carried by a sail, with the motto *Festina lente*, meaning "hasten slowly"; or alternatively the motto *Ut tollar uno*: to free oneself from the weight of the earth, one needed the sail of ingenuity.

Despite the vicissitudes of his family, the deaths of his sons Garzia and Giovanni and his wife Eleonora of Toledo, Cosimo did not for a moment abandon his project of creating a great nation. In vain did he try to justify a dynastic chain by calling himself 'second duke', and in vain did he claim to be a legitimate sovereign. In reality, the Council had merely presented him to the Emperor for his choice: he had merely obeyed the orders. "Charles V felt that he had already done a great deal by plucking an unknown young man from obscurity and entrusting him with an important government".[63] There was a gulf between this and his investiture as king that the Spanish monarch never thought to bridge. Thus, Cosimo had no choice but to show respect for his role as vassal and to renounce his traditional friendship with France in order to faithfully follow the emperor in the meanders

62 Ibid., p. 130.

63 Maurice Andrieux, *I Medici*, Dall'Oglio, Milano 1978, p. 478.

of his policy, both against Francis I and the Pope.

When Charles V abdicated in favour of his brother Ferdinand in 1555, Cosimo hoped for a more favourable situation, but the new emperor showed no particular interest in the Tuscan kingdom, even after the Treaty of Cateau-Cambrésis (1559), by which France renounced its ambitions in Italy.

Cosimo then turned to the Holy See, the only authority that could legitimise his dynasty. Having re-established good relations with the Vatican, he initially confined himself to asking for a cardinal's hat for his son Giovanni, which the Pope readily granted. Giovanni soon died of malaria (1562) and the Pope again rushed to give the hat to his brother Ferdinand, who was still a boy.

Finally, in 1569, the time had come. While all the great powers were preoccupied and distracted by the religious wars that were raging in Europe, a papal bull from Pope Pius V granted Cosimo the title of Grand Duke of Tuscany, with the concession of hereditary sovereignty. The pope was arrogating to himself imperial prerogatives, but the timing was right and no one objected. The Emperor himself finally agreed, also because his sister Joanna of Austria had married Francesco, Cosimo's son and future heir to the Grand Duchy. Cosimo had finally achieved for himself and his son the affinity with the imperial family that he had longed for. On 8 March 1570, in Rome, he received from the Pope the Grand Ducal sceptre and crown, decorated with the Florentine red lily. The Grand Duke's crown was engraved with the inscription: BENEFICIO PII V PONT. MAX. confirming that the election was directly dependent on the Pope. "The Medici had finally reached the highest peaks and the royal crown rested on their heads. One hundred and seventy years after Giovanni di Bicci, the humble banker of Florence, his descendant entered the ranks of European monarchs".[64]

In a praising epigram prepared for his coronation, Cosimo was

64 G. F. Young, "I Medici", cit., p. 615.

described not as a Florentine but as an Etruscan, the third ruler after the mythical Janus and the historical Porsenna: «Me Ianus tenuit primus, Porsenna secundus, tertius hetrusco Cosmus in arte regit». This was in spite of the profound political differences between the Grand Duchy and the ancient Etruscan confederation, the perception of which was still influenced by the falsifications of Annio da Viterbo. But in practice it was the evocation of the passage of a mythological heritage.

The first Grand Duke of Tuscany and Etruria, on his death (1574), left his heirs a rich and prestigious country. The comparison between an uncertain past and a flourishing present shows the historical dimension of Cosimo, who was able to assert himself and rule, the protagonist of a firm and wise policy. Florence and Tuscany owe him their astonishing economic recovery.

The new "lucumone" died on 21 April 1574, at the age of fifty-five, after thirty-seven years of reign, wrapped in the mantle of the Order of Santo Stefano, which he had founded, and buried with his sword, his sceptre, his necklace of the Order of the Golden Fleece[65] and his Grand Ducal crown. "*The theory of Cosimo, slowly and painstakingly built up, had survived the death of its author and its influence would be long and lasting in the years to come*".[66]

At that time Tuscany coincided ideally with Etruria[67] and tombstones appeared throughout the country on which the word "Etruriae" still appears next to the word "dux".

Together with Pier Vettori, Giovan Battista Adriani (1511-1579) was the official orator at the commemoration of Cosimo's

---

65 In Italian *Ordine del Toson D'Oro*. One of the most important European orders of chivalry, modelled on the English Order of the Garter. It was created in 1430 by Philip III of Burgundy to celebrate his marriage to the Portuguese princess Isabella of Aviz.

66 G. Cipriani, "Il mito etrusco...", cit., p. 112.

67 Without the Republic of Lucca. Cosimo did not hide the fact that Lucca, along with Siena, was part of his programme of territorial conquests. The Lucchese Francesco Burlamacchi, fearing for his city, hatched a plan to break the Medici hegemony over Tuscany, with the collaboration of Cosimo's usual adversaries: Piero and Leone Strozzi. The plot failed with the capture and murder of Burlamacchi (1548).

death, during which the illustrious deceased's existence was linked to the Etruscan heritage. Adriani, a man of letters and a man of arms, had already dedicated to the Duke the 22-volume *Istoria dei suoi tempi*, in which the myth of the superiority of Florence and the triumph of the whole of Tuscany merged.

Linguistic studies after the conquest of Siena

During the years of the conflict with Siena, studies had accelerated, while the appearance and restoration of new finds, including the great bronzes, astonished and confirmed the greatness of the Etruscans. The research of great men of letters such as Varchi, Segni and Salviati could now bear more mature fruit, also because an Etruscan territorial unit had already been conquered and it did not seem necessary to force the idea with fantasy.

This realism was already present in the figure of Benedetto Varchi, whose Storie Fiorentine, written in the years of Cosimo's reign, was not published until the 18th century. Divided into 16 books (from 1527 to 1538), the text is not short of politically 'embarrassing' events and witty analyses. Varchi's style was innovative and could be described as journalistic, as he paid great attention to the refutation of sources.

In 1570 the *Hercolano* was published posthumously, written at the height of Cosimo's reign (when it was already circulating as a manuscript). The work affirms the importance of the Florentine vernacular, arguing that the Italian language must be the living language of a people and not that of courtly literati. The treatise consists of a dialogue between Varchi himself and Count Ercolano, in which they discuss whether the Greek language is richer or less rich than our vernacular. Varchi took the opportunity to list hundreds of Florentine expressions, all related to 'favellare', none of which had a Greek equivalent! The work pleased Cosimo and the lovers of Tuscan things, and also proved that the Etruscans had

STORIE
FIORENTINE
DI MESSER
BERNARDO SEGNI,
GENTILUOMO FIORENTINO,
Dall'Anno MDXXVII. al MDLV.
Colla Vita
di
NICCOLO' CAPPONI,
Gonfaloniere della Repubblica di
Firenze, deſcritta dal medeſimo SEGNI
ſuo Nipote.

IN AUGUSTA MDCCXXIII.
Appreſſo DAVID RAIMONDO MERTZ,
e
GIO. JACOPO MAJER.

Frontispiece of the Florentine Histories by Bernardo Segni, from a splendid 18th-century edition, with engraving depicting the 'Florentine Gentleman'.

put their stamp on the vernacular before the Greeks and Romans (as in the case of the "aspiration" typical of Tuscan pronunciation).

According to Varchi, the classics of the fourteenth century were not sufficient to complete the new literary language, and it was therefore necessary to draw on the vernacular, especially the Florentine language. This was a significant advance on the assumptions proposed by Pietro Bembo, on whom Varchi's own studies were based. An example of this tendency can be found in an answer the scholar gave to Benvenuto Cellini, who had asked him to improve the style of his own biography. Varchi advised him "*... to leave it as it was, in the first and true draft*".[68]

Meanwhile, the activities of individual scholars, the Accademia and the Studio were joined by new institutions. Some have survived to the present day, such as the Accademia della Crusca, founded

---

68 This is taken from a letter from Cellini dated 22 May 1559, reported by Ettore Camesasca in *Dizionario Biografico degli Italiani*, 1979, vol. XXIII.

by Leonardo Salviati (1540-1589), a pupil of Varchi's, under the duchy of Francesco I. Salviati was already an active researcher in the last years of Cosimo's government and the author of l'*Orazione in lode della fiorentina lingua* (1564), a veritable manifesto of linguistic policy in which he sought to reconcile the differences between spoken and literary language.

Noah shows his sons the twelve cities of Etruria. Palazzo del Comune, Viterbo.

The Great Bronzes

During the reign of Cosimo I, thanks to the duke's passionate interest, Etruscan masterpieces such as *Minerva*, *Chimera* and *Arringatore* were brought to Florence from Tuscany and still represent the excellence of Etruscan bronzes in the Medici collections. The statues found in the 16th century were used by the Medici family as examples to mythologise the Etruscan past and justify contemporary attempts at unification. The 'bronzes' on display at the National Archaeological Museum in Florence are called 'great' for many reasons, not just because they are life-size (or slightly smaller) statues.

Minerva and the Medici Gorgon

Minerva, daughter of Jupiter, who gave birth to her from his own head without female intervention (after absorbing Metis, her mother), is the goddess of wisdom, industrious human labour and defensive warfare. Such a wide and important sphere of influence made the goddess highly venerated in Greece as well as in Etruria, where she appeared under the name of Menvre. It seems that the "goddess of a thousand tasks" entered the Roman cult during the reign of the Tarquins (of Etruscan origin) and that, together with Jupiter and Juno, she formed the Capitoline triad, analogous to the Etruscan celestial triad. However, according to Pauly-Wissowa[69], the Roman Minerva was not of Etruscan origin, but of Italic origin, from the town of Faleri. From here she would have passed into Etruscan and then Roman worship.

The "Cosmian" *Minerva* was found in 1541 in Arezzo, near the church of San Lorenzo, during the excavation of a well. Made of lost wax bronze and 1.55 metres high, it must have adorned

69 Pauly-Wissova, *Enciclopedia Reale dell'antichità classica*, 1978.

The Minerva found in Arezzo. Drawing by P&A

the room of a domus belonging to a wealthy Arezzo family in the 1st century A.D., since archaeological excavations in the area have revealed rooms decorated with mosaics and marble inlays. When it was discovered, Cosimo was immediately informed and wanted the statue in Florence. In 1559 it was placed with other antiquities in the Scrittoio di Calliope in Palazzo Vecchio, famous for the ceiling painting of the Muse by Giorgio Vasari.

Minerva to the Uffizi

In 1782, the antiquary of the Galleries, Luigi Lanzi, exhibited *Minerva* together with the other great bronzes of the Florentine collections (the *Chimera*, the *Arringatore* and the *Idolino of Pesaro*) in the Corridor of the Mezzogiorno of the Uffizi Gallery. It remained there until 1890, when, following the creation of the Royal Central Museum of Etruscan Civilization (then the National Archaeological Museum), it was transferred with the other bronzes to the Palazzo della Crocetta.

The original state of the artefact is unclear, as it had already undergone bronze, plaster and wood restorations in the 16th century, the extent of which is uncertain.

The lower part of the figure has undergone extensive restorations, particularly the right arm, which was added in bronze from the shoulder in 1785 by the sculptor Francesco Carradori. The pose of the arm shows Minerva in an oratorical movement reminiscent of that of the *Arringatore*. This pose also had a choreographic explanation, since in the new Uffizi exhibition the two statues were placed opposite each other.

In the ancient prototype, the arm was probably stretched across the bust, the forearm raised and bent at the elbow to hold a spear, a recurring attribute of the warrior goddess we see here armed with the raised Corinthian helmet decorated with an owl (another attribute of the goddess) and a small snake.

Minerva appears dressed in a long peplos that reaches her feet, to which she wears high sandals. She also wears a *himation*, i.e. a cloak that covers one shoulder and wraps around her waist, descending to her knee. On her chest she wears the ègida (a breastplate) made of snake scales and edged with serpents, in the centre of which is a lucky charm medallion with a representation of a flattened face, with chubby cheeks, of a small Gorgon.

Cosimo was not unfamiliar with the image of Medusa's head, which had retained a strong symbolic value in the Middle Ages and Renaissance. Already Giuliano de' Medici had had himself represented in a bust with armour bearing a Gorgon's head. Cosimo I would have himself portrayed with the same sign by Benvenuto Cellini, in imitation of the Roman emperors, just a few years after the *Minerva* was found.

The Artemis was recovered together with other small bronzes that also found their way into the Medici collections but whose traces were soon lost. Recently, some of them have been identified with some of the small bronzes on display at the Archaeological Museum in Florence. These are a young offerer, a griffin and a bearded man with a patera. The griffin is an attribute of Tinia, the highest divinity of the Etruscan pantheon, and its presence reinforces the idea that the group comprising the *Chimera* belonged to a votive stipe dedicated to the god, as suggested by the dedication in Etruscan characters engraved on the leg of the *Chimera* itself.

The work is not a Greek original from the classical period (as Winckelmann believed), nor is it a Roman copy of a Hellenistic variant. Twenty-five statues are known, all of which can be traced back to the so-called Athena Vescovali, once held in Rome in the eponymous collection and now in the Hermitage in St. Petersburg. These derive from a Praxitelian model, possibly the Athena of Mantinea sculpted in the 4th century BC.

However, if this Artemis is based on a Hellenistic variant of the Vescovali model, it differs from the other copies both for stylistic reasons (favouring a certain calligraphy and a simpler layout) and because it is the only existing bronze copy.

It is not possible to determine whether the *Minerva* is the work of an Etruscan workshop. It could have come from Arezzo, which was an important centre of the metallurgical industry: In 205 BC, Arezzo was the only Etruscan city to supply Scipio with weapons in significant numbers.

Only a few pieces of Arezzo's rich bronze production have survived, the wreckage of a real shipwreck, considering the fame of the Etruscans as bronze workers in the ancient world. From Volsini alone, according to Pliny, no less than two thousand statues were brought to Rome after the expulsion by the Romans (264 BC)![70]

---

70 Plinio, *Naturalis Historia*, XXXIV,34.

The Chimera of Arezzo. Drawing by P&A.

The Chimera of Arezzo

Another important find, second in chronological order but more important in an absolute sense, was the bronze *Chimera of Arezzo*. Chimera, whose name literally means "goat" in Greek, raged in the region of Lycia, according to myth. It had the body and head of a lion, a serpentine tail and a goat's head in the middle of its back; it spewed flames from its mouth, burning crops and reducing those who approached to ashes. The hero Bellerophon, flying over the monster on Pegasus, thrust his spear into its jaws and killed it. This episode is often depicted in Etruscan art, for example on an urn that can still be seen in the Archaeological Museum in Florence.

The discovery of the statue dates back to 1552-1553, when the new Medici fortifications were being built in Arezzo. Outside the gate of San Lorentino, on the road to Florence, several bronzes were found, including the *Chimera*. For the Medici, this discovery immediately took on great spiritual and political significance. The statue was quickly transported to Florence, where it remained for a long time in the Palazzo Vecchio, in the Leo X room, and only much later, in 1718, was it transferred to the Uffizi Gallery.

According to tradition, the front and hind legs of the left side of the animal were restored by Benvenuto Cellini with the help of Cosimo I himself; while the tail, lost or broken, was restored by Francesco Carradori in 1785. The original tail was meant to pounce menacingly on Bellerophon, not to bite off a horn from the goat's head: the original iconography can be seen on some Greek coins preserved in the "Medagliere" of the Museo Archeologico in Florence, presumably part of the Grand Ducal Collections.

Like the hollow-cast *Minerva*, the statue of the *Chimera* presents archaic elements such as the mane, which is resolved by schematic flame-shaped curls, or the lion-like muzzle, similar to Greek models from the 5th century BC, while the body appears austere and slender. The sculpture captures the moment when the beast is pierced by the spear and the goat's head is about to fall back, almost in agony. The lion's jaws and the bristling fur on its neck show all the rage and aggression of the wounded but not yet succumbing animal, its body arched and snarling with ferocity. The work dates from the heyday of the Classical period and shows the substance, but the stylisation of the details, with almost decorative modules, takes us back to the archaic tradition.

This mixture is typical of Etruscan taste in the first half of the 4th century B.C., and comparison with contemporary funerary lions from Val Vidone and Vulci has led to the conclusion that the work is strictly Etruscan and that it was cast between 380 and 360 B.C..

It is likely that the statue was part of a group that included a reproduction of Bellerophon riding Pegasus, but it cannot be excluded that it was a votive offering in its own right. This hypothesis seems to be confirmed by the presence of an inscription on the right front paw, engraved before the Despite the fame of this important find, the presence of the statue caused disquiet among the population: it was said that the *Chimera* would bring bad luck to its owner and to the city that guarded it. Perhaps it was because of this legend that Cosimo, after keeping the statue in the Palazzo Vecchio, had it moved to the Villa of Castello, in the immediate north-west of Florence.

One of the first French tourists to visit Florence, Michel de Montaigne, described it in his Journal du Voyages (1580-81): "... *in a room of this prince's palace, on a pillar, represented in bronze in its natural state, there is a strange four-legged animal, the front of which is entirely scaled, and on the back of which, I know not what kind of members, like horns, are to be seen. They say it was found in a cave in the mountains of the country and brought down alive some years ago*".[71]

Aulus Metellus, the Arringer

The bronze work known as the *Arringatore*, dating from the end of the second century BC, was found between Perugia and Lake Trasimeno in 1556.[72] It was secretly introduced within the Tuscan borders and sold to Cosimo I.

The figure is life-size (m. 1.70), elegantly draped, with one arm extended towards her listeners. She seems to herald the synthesis of realism in late Etruscan portraiture in the rigour of her expression and the tension of her gestures.

---

71 Michel de Montaigne, *Viaggio in Italia*, Laterza, Roma-Bari 1991, p.139.

72 According to one tradition, the find took place in the fields near Sanguineto on Lake Trasimeno, where the battle between the Romans and Hannibal's troops took place, and then was moved to Pila, near Perugia.

The Arringer. Drawing by P&A

This authoritative figure wears the "toga exigua" and high shoes. With his gesture he seems to attract the attention of the spectators in order to prepare himself for the sermon ("silentium manu facere"). The right hand (which was broken off when the statue was found) is larger than the rest of the body, in order to emphasise the gesture. This device, known to Michelangelo and his contemporaries, creates a preferred view from a slightly offset position to the right.

The statue is hollow-cast in seven parts, worked separately and then joined together; the legs are cast in one piece for greater stability. The rendering of the drapery shows the skill of the sculptor, although there are some anatomical uncertainties, especially in the joint of the right shoulder. The upward movement of the folds and the slant of the pose draw attention to the gesture and the face, which rests on a high neck and is moved by long, hollow wrinkles on the forehead. The cheeks are flattened and the lips are tight and skilfully drawn.

A few subtle incisions on the sides of the eyes create the effect of senility. The eye sockets, once filled with glass paste, prepare the sharp expressiveness of the gaze. The hair is chiselled into regular curls and glued to the skull, with the exception of the low fringe, which is slightly raised.

The gesture of the person represented in the statue, as well as the clothing, make our subject a Roman citizen, although Etruscan by birth, as confirmed by the inscription in Etruscan language engraved on the lower edge of the toga. The statue would represent the moment of the cultural, social and political Romanisation of Etruria.

The inscription on the toga tells us that the statue was dedicated to the god Tece Sansl, a "father god" figure worshipped on the shores of Lake Trasimeno. It reads: "AULESI METELIS VE VESIAL CLENSI CEN FLERES TECE SANSL TENINE TUTHINE CHISVLICS": "To Aulus Metellus, son of Vel and Vesia, this statue was dedicated in gratitude to the god Tece Sansl, with the sacred rites and all the prescribed devotions". Piero Bernardini Marzolla, on the other hand, relying on alleged correspondences between the Etruscan and Sanskrit languages, came up with the following translation: "To Aulus Metellus, son of Vel and Vesia, the assembly erected this statue, thanks to the payment of a public contribution".[73]

73 The bronze statue would represent a person who died in the battle of Trasimeno that took place in the previous century (217 BC), enforced by the descendants of his family. For the translation see Piero Bernardini Marzolla, *L'Etrusco una lingua ritrovata*, Mondadori, Milan 1984, TLE 651 pp. 149 ff.

Benvenuto Cellini, Perseus. Loggia dei Lanzi, Florence.

The artists and the great bronzes

The rediscovery of the Etruscan bronzes aroused great interest among artists, and one senses that there was a debate about these works, their restoration and their role in refuting the Etruscan-Cosimian spirit. The reinterpretation of the theme of the "Etruscan Chimera" would never cease, as is shown by the numerous reworkings, from Renaissance drawings to contemporary copies (that of Primo Aglietti in Arezzo, or Arturo Martini's Lion of

Donatello, Judith and Holofernes, copy on display in Piazza della Signoria.

Monterosso, in which the same animal appears in a different position).

The *Minerva* and the Arringer were also copied and reinterpreted in institutional contexts (furnishing of institutions, courts and palaces of power) and later in contemporary artistic contexts (think of a work by Michelangelo Pistoletto in which the reproduction of Aule Metellus appears in a mirror, brushing against his reflection with his raised arm). It is therefore "Etruscan statuary" in the broadest sense that is cyclically affirmed.

Vasari already used the *Chimera* as an example to recognise Etruscan art. Of this origin of the work he is "*most certain, and I say this not because I found it in Arezzo, my country, to give it greater praise, but because it is true; and because I have always been of the opinion that the art of sculpture began to flourish in Tuscany at that time; and it seems to me that Chimera proves it, because the hair, which is the most difficult thing in sculpture, is better expressed by the Greeks, even if the Latins did it perfectly in Rome; for which this animal, which is also large, and the fleeces of his own that he wears beside his neck, are more awkward than the Greeks did to him, for it seems that the Etruscans knew less about it, as those who, having begun to know about art in more recent times, have not yet found the true way; and this is shown by those Etruscan letters that he has in his upright paw* (...)"[74]

In another passage of the *Ragionamenti*, Vasari recognises the value of the expressiveness of Etruscan art and deduces the iconography of Bellerophon: "*There is the evidence in the medals in the possession of my Lord Duke, which came from Rome, and which have the head of a goat stuck on the neck of this lion, which, as Your Excellency sees, also has the belly of a snake; and we have found the broken tail among these fragments of bronze with so many metal figures (...), and these wounds that she has on her prove it, and also the pain that is seen in the readiness that is in the head of this animal, and it seems to me that this master has expressed it well*".[75]

From the author's observations and contemporary drawings, we know that the tail was missing at the time of discovery, and that the legs were present but damaged. Cellini would therefore not have altered the work significantly during the restoration. As mentioned, Carradori intervened much later, who in the 18th century played an important role in the preservation of Tuscan antiquities, particularly in the case of the *Minerva*. He was the restorer of the famous Medici Vase and other sculptures kept in the Uffizi, bringing to the artisan tradition of restoration the legacy of centuries of sculptural progress. In the Villa Borghese and the Galatea Gallery (Rome), the artist also carried out decorations with faux columns that recall Tuscan interiors and Italian taste.

74 Vasari, *Ragionamenti*, 1588, gio. I, rag. III, *Sala di Giovanni, Principe e Giorgio.*

75 Ibidem.

However, Florentine bronze work reached its virtuoso peak precisely in the years of the great archaeological discoveries and the most daring studies of Etruscan mythical and linguistic origins, when Cosimo was preparing to conquer Siena and scholars such as Giambullari, Varchi and Segni were carrying out their most important studies.

Between 1545 and 1554, Benvenuto Cellini began working on *Perseus* after seeing *Minerva*, only to complete it in the years following the appearance of the *Chimera*, about which he wrote in his autobiography.[76]

The work is a summation of a multitude of symbolic elements and stylistic solutions in which the artist makes a definitive programmatic effort. The decision to work in bronze was also influenced by the fame of the Great Bronzes. The raised arm of Perseus, holding the head of Medusa, is immediately familiar to us, recalling the figures of *Minerva* or the *Arringatore*; and in its own way claims the role of the Etruscan duchy in history. In fact, the choice of mythological theme seems to celebrate the victory of the Medici over the Republican experience. We are faced with a synthesis of the Florentine sculptural tradition, which includes the monumentality of Michelangelo's David and the energetic realism of Donatello.

In those years, working in bronze also meant celebrating the Etruscan heritage, and the reference to mythology was therefore automatic. The examples are numerous: from Giambologna's *Mercury* (conceived in 1550), which cannot fail to recall the dancing figures of ancient frescoes, to Vincenzo Danti's *Beheading of St John the Baptist* (1570), in which Salome wears a bodice similar to that of Minerva and the executioner takes the weapon, the charge and the hair of Perseus.

Apart from this, and ignoring the many examples of bold mannerist fusions, Renaissance bronzes had already been

76 Benvenuto Cellini, *Vita di Sé Medesimo*, Cocchi, 1728, t. II, p. 321.

developing an awareness of a relationship with antiquity for almost a century. Donatello, as an absolute forerunner, explained in *Judith and Holofernes* (1453-1457) his attraction to the bas-reliefs of Etruscan urns, the style and quadrature of which are reproduced in the podium of the bronze statue, which already recalls the poses of the great Etruscan figures to be discovered in

Giambologna, Equestrian statue of Ferdinand I. Piazza SS. Annunziata, Florence.

the following decades. And in Ghiberti's *St Matthew* (1420-1423), we could see the posture of the *Arringer*; and in the bas-reliefs of the baptistery, the framing of ancient urns; while in the pedestal of Pollaiolo's *Hercules at Rest* (1480), the Hellenistic sphinxes and the paws of the *Chimera*, destined to spread also in the motifs of Florentine furnishings. This would be a phenomenon of great aesthetic coincidence between antiquity and modernity: a kind of syncretism. We can also speculate that artists and scientists saw in bronze a value linked to alchemical and neo-Platonic assumptions, in the attainment of the value of the "pure idea".

It would thus be Ferdinando de' Medici who would celebrate his father Cosimo I with the equestrian monument visible today in Piazza Signoria. This was commissioned to Giambologna, who would combine in a single work the splendour of Etruscan bronzes and the equestrian tradition already expressed by Donatello in Padua with the monument to Gattamelata.

Finally, Ferdinand himself will appear on horseback as a condottiere in the large bronze in Piazza SS. Annunziata, also by Giambologna.

Francis, Ferdinand and the Etruscans

With Francis and Ferdinand, "Greater Etruria" would continue to grow, and Etruscological studies would gain awareness, slowly moving beyond mythological-historical fantasies.

Francis, more than his father, had a scholarly bent. He was curious about natural history, a student of alchemy and, from a young age, a collector and restorer of small bronzes, Etruscan-Roman vases and rarities of all kinds. He became a duke in 1574, and in 1576 the Emperor Maximilian II granted him the title of Grand Duke of Tuscany on a permanent basis, ignoring the papal bull that had raised Cosimo to this dignity. With the birth of the male heir Philip (1577), the continuity of the dynasty was now assured, and Francis proceeded to consolidate his own learning and power.

Philip was born under the best of auspices: the Etruscan myth guaranteed his authority, and the support of Rome and Spain was assured. In 1577, Pierio Fontani of Fermo, in his *Tages ad Franciscum Medicem Magnum Etruriae Ducem*, had linked the splendour of the aedes deorum with ancient Etruscan religiosity - an example of the boundless mythologising of the new Etruria and the Medici "lucumoni"! Unfortunately, the child did not reach adulthood. Weak and sickly, he died on 29 March 1582, ending any hope of a legitimate succession.

Fontani linked the Medici directly to the ancient Etruscan civilisation, so much so that any historical distinction no longer seemed to make sense. The Medici were presented not as the heirs of a distant greatness, but as Etruscans in their own right, destined by fate to increase the prestige and power of their people. Present and past merged again in ideological symbolism, «and it was precisely Tuscany, recently united into a Grand Duchy, that emerged victorious and triumphant, as if only with the consolidation of Medici power had it achieved a goal it had coveted and awaited for centuries».[77] Traditionally associated with Tarquinia, from which he would have taken his name, the young Taiges was taken to Fiesole, where he convened a meeting of the twelve Etruscan kings. Here he gave precise instructions for rituals and practised the art of predicting the future, shortly announcing the coming birth of the great Florence and the rise of the Medici.[78]

But Francis's success had already been extolled by Michael Capri and others, who even compared him to the Etruscan Porsenna.[79]

Through his ministers, the new Duke continued Cosimo's policies, but despite some successes, the Tuscan economy seemed to have been affected by the recent war efforts. Moreover, the war of Philip II, King of Spain, against Portugal forced the Florentine ally to send a contingent of four thousand men and other aid, which weakened the finances. Shortly afterwards, a serious epidemic known as "Male del Castrone" struck Tuscany and beyond;[80] agricultural shortages caused by two years of poor harvests were the cause of its rapid spread. The measures taken by the Magistrate of Plenty were hardly enough to calm the discontented population of

Vincenzo Borghini in a portrait in the Biblioteca Nazionale Centrale in Florence. (Sailko cc.3.0)

77 G. Cipriani, "Il mito etrusco…", cit., p. 129. L'opera del Fontani è analizzata da p. 123 e seg.

78 *Ibid.*, p. 126.

79 Michele Capri, *Canzone al Serenissimo Cosimo Medici Gran Duca di Toscana*, Sermartelli, Firenze 1570, *cfr.* G. Cipriani, "Il mito etrusco…", cit., p. 115 e seg.

80 The "cast diesase". This is a malignant epidemic cough (mala tussis) accompanied by influenza.

the capital.

But the propaganda of Etruscan Tuscany did not stop. In 1583, Agostino Fortunio, a priest from Fiesole, mentioned Noah's / Giano again in his *Cronichetta*: "*So Noah filled the world with new colonies and taught the people how to cultivate the land and plant vineyards, he was called by them "Iano", which in their language means viniferous and vitiferous*".[81] The most imaginative legends were reaffirmed to celebrate the antiquity and the wealth of Tuscany, taking up those political aspects that had previously so effectively expressed the needs of the new Magni Duces Aetruriae: Noah had not only ennobled Tuscany and Italy, but had also shown the best and most dignified form of government: that of the monarchy.

Vincenzo Borghini and the overthrow of the Aramean thesis

Despite numerous legendary reconstructions over more than a century, a group of researchers had never ceased to doubt the mythological-semitic origins of the Etruscans. The Benedictine Vincenzo Borghini (1515-1580) had railed against «Talmudists and Aramaeans»[82] mocking Annio and Postel but his refutations were not published for many years. In his treatise *Dell'origine della città di Firenze*, published posthumously in 1584 (under the title *Discorsi*), Borghini argued that Florence was a Roman colony and had little in common with the ancient Arameans.

Borghini did not deny the existence and greatness of the Etruscan people, but he wanted to express himself in historically reliable terms and downplay any fantasy. Livy, Pliny, Strabo and Dionysius of Halicarnassus were his main sources, which he used extensively to define the origins of the "Tuscan Empire", now under the aegis of the Medici. The glories of the past constituted

---

81 From the *Cronichetta del Monte San Savino di Toscana* (1583), dedicated to Grand Duke Francesco de' Medici, Libro Primo, p. 2.

82 *Dell'origini della città di Firenze*, in *Discorsi di Monsignor Don Vincenzo Borghini*, Viviani, Firenze 1755, parte I, p. 16.

The entrance to the Villa Reale in Castello (Florence), the current seat of the Accademia della Crusca.

only one part of an absolutely real Florentine history, such as that narrated by Scipione Ammirato.[83]

In fact, Borghini's figure is known for his tendency towards "philological restoration", which will be oriented mainly on Dante studies and the role of allegory in the interpretation of the texts of the supreme poet, with a prudence in criticism and judgement that will unite the approach to literature as well as to historical data.

The birth of the Accademia della Crusca

In the last two decades of the sixteenth century, in a climate of greater scientific awareness and with the prejudices of propaganda largely overcome, the ground was prepared for the foundation of the Accademia della Crusca, to which we owe the creation of the

83 The Istoria Fiorentina was published in Florence in 1600, the year before the author's death.

Francis I in a portrait in which he appears with an ancient statue.

vocabulary and the definitive establishment of the "Florentine" language.

One of the main promoters of the Academy was, from 1582, Leonardo Salviati, already known for his oration in praise of the Florentine language. Salviati was a member of the academy under the name of Infarinato and actively contributed to the popularisation of the Tuscan language.

He was largely responsible for the classical and purist direction of the Accademia della Crusca, which still follows his work today. Indeed, in the preface to the first edition of the Vocabolario della Crusca (1612), the academicians declared that they intended to follow Salviati's grammar and orthography.

In his *Orazioni*, Salviati reiterates one of the most important characteristics of the Florentine language: its spontaneous acceptance by foreigners and by many Italians who come to learn it, without finding the difficulties encountered in learning Latin. Thus, Etruria turns out to be "*the main seat, the eternal sanctuary, the founded temple... Rejoice therefore, magnificent city of your glorious exalted lily, rejoice eccelsa republic of your venerable name revived, rejoice noble province of your ancient crown recovered!*".[84]

The Grand Duchy of Ferdinand

In 1587, after the death of Francesco and Bianca Cappello, "*on the 25th of October, the Senate and the Council of Two Hundred, assembled in the great hall of the Ducal Palace, gave Ferdinand the solemn oath of obedience, and the people received him with great joy as Grand Duke of Tuscany.*"[85]

The Medici coat of arms consisted of red orbs on a field of gold, the number of which varied according to the period. But in addition to the family coat of arms, each member chose a personal insignia, consisting of a symbolic figure accompanied by a motto in Latin. As we read at the base of Ferdinand's equestrian monument in Florence's Piazza Santissima Annunziata, he chose an ingenious one. It consists of a swarm of bees with a queen bee at the centre, with the motto Maiestate tantum, "with royal dignity alone", which also means "without the imposition of force".

The Grand Duke thus promised to rule his subjects as the queen bee rules her hive, which obeys her not because she is powerful and overbearing, but because she is the mother and queen to whom the whole hive submits in loving discipline for the common good. The Medici kingship was indeed recognised and confirmed by both the Vatican and the Empire.

However, unlike the queen bee, who was abundantly nourished by the worker bees, Ferdinand did not want to tax the people in

84 *Orazione funerale del cavalier Lionardo Salviati, da lui publicamente recitata nelle esequie del Cosimo Medici, Gran Duca di Toscana*, Sermantelli, Firenze, 1574.

85 A. Ferrini, *Compendio di Storia della Toscana*, 1840, p. 160.

order to raise revenue. He preferred to earn his own money: the court of the Pitti palace also became a granary, a wine cellar, an olive press and much more. In 1590, when famine struck Tuscany, Lapini noted that "*by the grace of God and our Grand Duke, we have not yet lacked bread.*"[86]

The royal marriage of Francesco's daughter Maria de' Medici to Henry IV of France, celebrated by proxy in Florence in October 1600, consecrated the rank and power of the third Grand Duke of Etruria.

By this time the Medici had forged even closer ties with all the major nobles, a recognition of their weight in the European sphere. The importance of the Grand Duchy was to be demonstrated by its participation in the Crusade against the Turks[87] and by the maritime expedition to 'America', organised by Sir Robert Dudley (Captain of the Port of Livorno) across the Atlantic to what is now Brazil. Unfortunately, the attempt to colonise a territory called 'New Etruria' failed, first because of the opposition of the Duke of Lerma (a favourite of the Spanish emperor Philip III) and then because of the death of Ferdinand, who had been so keen on the mission.

In an age so passionate about gossip, inventions, successes and failures, it would have been a great sourcc of pride for the Grand Dukes if the Etruscan myth had reached the other side of the ocean![88]

---

86 Agostino Lapini, "Diario fiorentino..." cit., p. 118.

87 The Order of the Knights of St. Stephen founded by Cosimo took on a remarkable development under Ferdinand I, with daring exploits that renewed the splendour of the ancient maritime republic of Pisa. The Tuscan fleet led by Admiral Jacopo Inghirami, after a few setbacks, achieved an important victory over the Turks in Bona, in 1608 and another the following year in the Tuscan archipelago.

88 The enterprise had been prepared at the beginning of 1608 and had seen the departure from Livorno of a galleon and a tartana laden with bales and goods, armed to withstand any attack and ready to cross the Atlantic. The command was given to a character who could find his place in the pages of a Salgari novel: Robert Thornton, a privateer who lived in 'free' Livorno, where many ex-convicts served out their crimes in the service of the Grand Duchy. The small fleet was to reach the northern coast of Brazil and then move inland. The main purpose of the mission was to prove to Europe that the Grand Duchy was capable of undertaking a colonial venture. There was also the possibility of bringing home any gold that might be found in the rumoured rich mines of Brazil.

Tourists buying antiquities in a print by Henry Tresham (c. 1790).

Seventeenth-century collecting and Inghirami's forgeries

At the beginning of the seventeenth century, the Etruscan myth was redefined, as can be seen from the trends in collecting, which brought Rome back to the fore, even in Tuscany. But even the collections of Cosimo I, after 1560, were directed towards Roman monuments and statues. In the *Arringatore*, for example, there was a tendency to recognise Seneca or Scipio and not the Etruscan figure to whom the inscriptions on the statue referred. The study of ancient and therefore Etruscan monuments was the prerogative of scholars and artists.

Among these, Carlo Roberto Dati (1619-1676), known as the "Etruscan Varro", stood out for his extensive knowledge of texts. He was the secretary of the Accademia della Crusca, to which we

---

Thornton sailed for almost a year, landing in Guyana and Brazil, exploring the Amazon and the mouth of the Orinoco, and calling at Trinidad. But when he returned to Livorno in July 1609, he found no authority to receive him because the Grand Duke had died and in Florence there was no longer any thought of establishing a trading colony overseas. Some natives captured on the Brazilian coast were brought to Florence to impress the Florentines, but in a short time five of them died of smallpox. One of them went on to live at the Medici court.

owe the third edition of the Vocabolario; like other scholars of his time, he was interested not only in the classics and the ancient world, but also in the popular language, from which he collected some bizarre forms and mottos in *Lepidezze di spiriti bizzarri e curiosi avvenimenti* (1829). He is also known for E*timologico toscano and Prose fiorentine* (1661). He worked on a large work, never completed, on the lives of ancient painters and other archaeological subjects.

Interest in this period was more antiquarian than scientific. The attention of collectors and scholars was focused not only on manuscripts, but also on ancient marbles, epigraphs, coins and precious stones. Rome and Florence were the centres of this cultural phenomenon. Among the protagonists of these collections was the Corsini family, who still display many epigraphs in the portico of their villa in Via del Prato (Florence). Many other epigraphs can still be seen in the cloister of the Medici-Riccardi palace.

The discovery of antiquities always brought fame to the cities where they were found. Curzio Inghirami (1614-1655), in order to promote the town of Scornello (ten kilometres from Volterra), where his family had a villa, invented from scratch antiquities, pseudo-Etruscan and pseudo-Latin epigraphs.[89]

The forgery was later exposed by Leone Allacci in 1640[90] and a treatise written by Inghirami himself in defence of his fantastic inventions was to no avail.[91]

89 Curzio Inghirami, *Ethruscarum antiquitatum fragmenta,* Francoforte 1637.

90 Leone Allacci, *Animadversiones in antiquitatum etruscarum fragmenta*, 1648.

91 Curzio Inghirami, *Discorso*, 1645.

The Eighteenth Century
Antiquities and Collecting

As mentioned above, interest in the Etruscans had already waned before the death of Ferdinando: Tuscan collecting was shifting back towards classical antiquity. However, subsequent Grand Dukes never ceased to acquire Etruscan relics and to boast the title "Magnus Dux Etruriae" on documents, plaques, medallions and even military cannons (many of these relics can be seen in the Bargello Museum).

During the twenty or so years he spent in Rome as Cardinal, Ferdinand bought all the classical sculptures that came his way, becoming the greatest collector in Rome. In his beautiful residence on the Pincio hill (purchased in 1576), he filled both the villa and the garden with a remarkable series of sculptures: the Medici Venus, found in the Villa Adriana in Tivoli, the Dancing Faun, the Wrestler, the Arrotino, the Apollino and the Group of Niobe, among others.

In the search for collectors' items, there was no shortage of excavations in Etruscan territory. In 1669, an archaeological campaign at the site of ancient Veio (curated by Abbot Falconieri on behalf of Cardinal Flavio Chigi) brought back a rich votive deposit of anatomical models, which ended up in the hands of Cardinal Leopoldo de' Medici and then passed into the family collection. It should therefore be emphasised that most of the finds from the Veio excavations, which were organised on the outskirts of Rome by scholars and collectors from the Roman milieu, were brought to Florence.

The success of the Etruscan myth only resumed vigorously from the 1720s, in a period of delicate transition between the exhaustion of the Medici dynasty and the rise of the Lorraine. The key event was the publication of Thomas Dempster's *De Etruria Regali*, which had remained unpublished since the previous century.

THOMÆ DEMPSTERI

DE

ETRURIA REGALI LIBRI VII.

NUNC PRIMUM EDITI

CURANTE

THOMA COKE

MAGNÆ BRITANNIÆ ARMIGERO

REGIÆ CELSITUDINI

COSMI III.

MAGNI DUCIS ETRURIÆ.

FLORENTIÆ. M.DCC.XXIII.

Title page of the Florentine edition of Thomas Dempster's De Etruria regali, *dedicated to Cosimo III in 1723.*

Montfaucon's journey

Bernard de Montfaucon (1655-1741) was received in Florence in 1700, during a stay in Italy described in the Diarium Italicum. Accompanied by Cardinal Francesco Maria, brother of Cosimo III, the French scholar visited the Medici collections.

The diary mentions some facts that reflect the direction of collecting at that historical moment; after admiring the statues, coins and precious stones in the collection, Montfaucon noted a large number of vases, fibulae, strigils and bronzes, which means that collectors were beginning to value them more highly. The Medici collection contained many Etruscan epigraphs, about which the scholar notes that hermeneutic attempts had not yielded good results because of the scarcity of material available to scholars.[92]

Even the testimony of Cosimo Della Rena (1615-1696), a member of the Crusca and an antiquarian who travelled between Rome and Florence, indicates the limited availability of artefacts that should have been made available to scholars: "*I had collected many fragments of Etruscan memoirs in order to compile a treatise; but as the years passed and I ran out of time, I was forced to appeal to the benevolent favour of the scholars of these subjects, so that by accumulating them with their own, they might take up their defence and not let them perish as fruitless and useless*".[93]

Montfaucon himself published 'L'antiquité expliquée et représentée en figures' in Paris between 1719 and 1724, a pictorial repertory of a large number of ancient monuments, including Etruscan ones.

Publication of Dempster's research

De Etruria Regali Libri Septem, the book written by Thomas Dempster (1579-1625), professor of law in Pisa, between 1616 and 1618, was finally published in Florence in 1723 with a dedication to Cosimo III and again in 1724 with a dedication to Gian Gastone. The fruit of great erudition and fertile imagination, this publication, although not a true scientific treatise, collected all the literary sources known at the time on the Etruscans.

Dempster's manuscript was first published thanks to the patronage of an English nobleman, Thomas Coke, 1st Earl of Leicester. The Earl was on his Grand Tour of Europe and had purchased the work from the Florentine scholar Anton Maria Salvini (1653-1729).

Officially commissioned by Grand Duke Cosimo II in 1615,

---

92 Bernard de Mountfacon, *Diarium Italicum*, Parigi 1702.

93 Cosimo Della Rena, *Della serie degli antichi duchi e marchesi di Toscana*, Firenze 1690, *cfr.* G. Morolli, "Vetus Etruria", cit., p. 125.

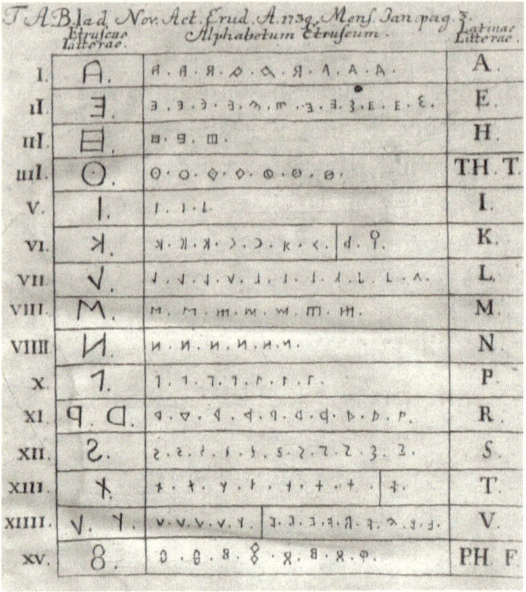

De Etruria Regali is a largely textual account of the history of early Tuscany. Accompanied by ninety-three engravings of Etruscan monuments, completed with notes and comments by the Florentine senator Filippo Buonarroti, the work was a new starting point for archaeological and historical research in Etruria. Also noteworthy are the linguistic observations, including those on the alphabet, which was recognised as 'of Greek type'.

TAB. I. ad Nov. Act. Erud. A. 1739. Mens. Jan. pag. 3.

Alphabetum Etruscum

	Latinae Litterae
I.	A.
II.	E.
III.	H.
IIII.	TH. T.
V.	I.
VI.	K.
VII.	L.
VIII.	M.
VIIII.	N.
X.	P.
XI.	R.
XII.	S.
XIII.	T.
XIIII.	V.
XV.	PH. F.

The Etruscan alphabet from Anton Francesco Gori's Museum Etruscum.

Thomas Dempster wrote in honour of the Medici family, who, according to tradition, were descended from the Etruscans, from whom they were said to have inherited wisdom and a taste for splendour. Once again, the text is intended to glorify the Grand Ducal family and does not hesitate to alter some scientific aspects. For example, the Etruscan word 'meddix' (magistrate?) is the surname of the great ruling family of Tuscany.

The success of the book was remarkable and of great political importance for Florence, regardless of the actual findings in the urban area, since it confirmed an image of the Medici and of Tuscany definitively linked to ancient Etruria.

This idea, which was still alive in the 18th century in Anton Francesco Gori's *Museum Etruscum* of 1737 (which we will discuss shortly), came through the fantasies of the Grand Tour and beyond into the collective imagination of tourism today.

The Accademia Colombaria

The historical and archaeological study of the Etruscans was well served by the Accademia Colombaria, which had been meeting in a bookseller's shop in Via del Corso since 1729. When the latter closed, Giovanni Girolamo de' Pazzi offered his palace in Borgo degli Albizzi, which was then called Palazzo Pazzi dell'Accademia Colombaria to distinguish it from the nearby Palazzo Pazzi della Congiura.

The Colombaria was officially born on 15 May 1735, when sixteen scholars began to record their erudite discussions. The academy took its name from the place where the lectures were held, the top floor of the Pazzi house, a dovecote-like tower overlooking the city. The first statutes of the Accademia were drawn up in the palace, and those who belonged to it took, ironically, a name related to pigeons (such as "Torraiolo", "Domestico", etc.). When meetings were held in the homes of other members, they were called 'posatoi'. The Accademia was located in Borgo degli Albizi until 1746, the year of Girolamo's death; after several moves, it finally found its current home in Via Sant'Egidio.

The *Colombi* ("Pigeons") also dealt with the presentation of Etruscan artefacts, manuscripts from different periods, inscriptions, coins and, in general, historical, philological and philosophical reports. In 1747 the first volume on the scientific activities of the Academy was published, followed by subsequent reports. Around the middle of the 18th century, research and publications slowed down considerably, only to pick up again in the following century, especially during the presidency of Gino Capponi, who reorganised the Academy, modernising it and limiting its research to the history of Tuscany.

The leading figure in the field of Etruscan studies and collecting was Anton Francesco Gori (1691-1757), one of the founders of the

Accademia Colombaria and curator of the *Museum Florentinum*, the great catalogue of Florentine collections. He was professor of history at the Studio Fiorentino and had close relations with philologists and humanists throughout Italy, as part of an open and harmonised vision of research.

Among Gori's most important publications is the *Museum Etruscum*, which describes a wide range of objects collected by Tuscan lords. Gori's interest in the Etruscans encouraged and strengthened the trend towards public collecting in the most diverse circles.

Further research in the Grand Duchy of Cosimo III and Giangastone

The Etruscan problem attracted the Verona historian and playwright Scipione Maffei (1675-1755), who moved to Florence in 1720 and was welcomed by Cosimo III and Giangastone, who encouraged him to study Etruscan epigraphy and antiquities.

Through the speculations contained in the text *Degl'Itali primitivi* in *Istoria Diplomatica* of 1727, Maffei starts from the Tables of Gubbio[94] to support the Canaanite origin of the Etruscans. Later, in *Trattato sopra la nazione etrusca e sopra gl'Itali primitivi*, published in 1739, he developed the hypothesis that the Etruscans were the true "Italians", from whom the Romans derived most of their civil and religious institutions. Also in this version of the theory, the Etruscans would be assimilated to the ancient Canaanites, hence the biblical origin of the Italic civilisation. It should be noted that, despite numerous refutations, the idea of a biblical-Semitic origin of the Etruscans was a "spectre" that was

---

94 These are seven bronze tablets found in the 15th century in Gubbio on which is engraved a text relating to complex ceremonial lustrations and expiations of the city. Datable to the 3rd-1st century B.C., they are undoubtedly inspired by traditions of an older era. Some are written in Umbrian characters and the Umbrian language, others in the Umbrian language and Latin alphabet. Table V is mostly written in Etruscan characters.

destined to reappear periodically in the studies of the Tuscans; we must bear in mind that archaeological science had not taken the necessary steps to definitively archive this "myth", which continued to represent an absolutely important link for the Medici.

After Gori's death, Giovan Battista Passeri (1694-1780) and Mario Guarnacci (1701-1785) became the main repositories of knowledge about Etruscan antiquities. The former elaborated new concepts both on the problem of language (for which he proposed an "inductive method"[95] that avoided the problems of the origin of the Etruscans) and on archaeological topics. We recommend his work in the three volumes *Picturae Etruscorum in vascoli*, published in 1767, a large illustrated collection of figurative ceramics from collections all over Italy, interpreted with a summary antiquarian method and superficially attributed to the Etruscans.

Instead, Mario Guarnacci concentrated his research on the territory from which he came: a member of one of Volterra's leading families, he had pursued an ecclesiastical career in Rome before retiring to his native town. In Volterra, between 1767 and 1772, he wrote *Origini italiche* (Italian Origins), a synthesis of the Etruscology of the time, with some advances, but also with fantastic-celebratory elements. He, too, proposed the old theories of the Annianes on the Jewish origin and the Etruscan primacy in European civilisation.

At this point, however, Guarnacci's position was anachronistic and not very sustainable. At the end of the eighteenth century, many scholars matured in an attitude of scepticism and weariness at the difficulty of framing the Etruscan world. If Etruria could still be of interest, it was above all as an example of a period of prosperity in the region, to be considered as a model for the present, in the context of the new reformist political positions. This was the approach taken by Giovanni Targioni Tozzetti (1712-1783),

95 A way of studying Etruscan through Etruscan itself, i.e. by comparing expressions used in different texts; this system would later be developed by Wilhelm Deecke in *Etruskische Forschungen*, I/IV, Stuttgart 1875-1880.

Giovan Battista Piranesi, romantic engraving (18th century).

progenitor of the great family of Tuscan naturalists, author of the reports of several journeys he made to various parts of Tuscany to observe its nature and civilisation. The scholar considered the pre-Roman past as a period of efficiency and development of productive structures in the region, in a regime of peaceful and autonomous cities.

Giovanni Maria Lampredi (1732-1793), a great jurist and theologian, also extolled the 'federal' regime of the Etruscan cities against the royal government, as did the Piedmontese Carlo Denina (1731-1813), an important figure in 18th-century Italian historiography, who in *Delle rivoluzioni d'Italia* described the pre-Roman period as a harmonious society governed by kings elected by the people and later with a 'federative' republican system.

Giovan Battista Piranesi

Roman scholars could not avoid looking at Etruria. Giovan Battista Piranesi (1720-1778) dealt with the Etruscans in two texts: *Magnificenza ed architettura dei Romani*, published in 1761,[96] and *Ragionamento apologetico in difesa dell'architettura egizia e toscana*, of 1769.[97]

Reviving the theories of the French abbot Jean-Jacques Barthélemy (the decipherer of the Phoenician language), Piranesi mixed real and imaginary elements on the Etruscan origin, but sensed the role of the Etruscans in the formation of Roman culture, asserting that their primacy was visible in the works of craftsmanship, especially in figurative ceramics. This led to a polemic with the "Greek revival" of Johann J. Winckelmann (1717-1768), whose *History of the Art of the Ancient World*, published in

The town of Cortona in an 18th century print.

96 Available in an edition edited by Antonio Giuliano. G. B. Piranesi, Della magnificenza ed architettura de' romani, Il Polifilo, Milan 1993.

97 Published in *Diverse maniere d'adornare i cammini ed ogni altra parte degli edifizi desunte dall'architettura Egizia, Etrusca e Greca con un Ragionamento Apologetico in defesa dell' architettura Egizia, e Toscana, opera del Cavaliere Giambattista Piranesi Architetto*, Parigi 1836.

1764, relegated the Etruscans to the role of mere suspender of Greek art.

At the same time, Winckelmann denounced how some paintings from Tarquinia were wasted by the air soon after the tomb was opened, and others were destroyed by graverobbers in the hope of finding some treasure. The antiquarian market had its own rude demands that disturbed the archaeological understanding of the Etruscans.

The birth of the Cortona Academy

The revival of interest in ancient Etruscan society found a response mainly in the Tuscan province, among members of the petty patriciate and the clergy, as a form of affirmation of urban identity and their own political and cultural role. This was particularly true during the period of uncertain transition between the Medici and Lorraine after the death of Anna Maria Ludovica de' Medici (1743).

On 29 December 1726, Abbot Onofrio Baldelli, with the help of three of his relatives, Ridolfino, Marcello and the young Filippo Venuti, founded the Etruscan Academy of Cortona, which contributed greatly to the development of the history of antiquity. Ridolfino's career in Rome, where he had established contacts with leading scholars and prominent figures in foreign colonies, contributed to the Academy's wealth and success, while Marcello settled in Naples and became librarian-conservator of the Archaeological Museum. Later Marcello had to return to Cortona to look after the family properties and the Academy.

As had been the case at the time of De Etruria Regali, which was characterized by pro-Medicean aims, so the activity that took place in the Academy of Cortona paid deference first to the Medici and immediately afterwards to Francis of Lorraine, referred to as the continuer of the splendors of the Etruria of the Lucumoni.

Skilful propaganda made the institution famous on the European stage, as Italian and foreign intellectuals joined it, including Montesquieu and Voltaire, attracted by Filippo Buonarroti, who had spent a long time in France.

A pleasant aspect of the Academy's activity was the exhumation of Etruscan names and ancient Etruscan customs. Every year a president was (and still is) elected, who was given the title of "lucumone". The first of these was Filippo Buonarroti. The Academy consisted of one hundred and forty members, forty of whom were citizens of Cortona and the others from other towns. The meetings were called "Coritane Nights": the bells of the Civic Palace rang out twice a month to summon the academicians, to which the women of the nobility were also invited.

This activity continued throughout the century and was documented in nine volumes published between 1738 and 1795. It is a real pleasure to leaf through the pages of these elegant volumes, entitled *Saggi di dissertazioni accademiche pubblicamente lette nella nobile Accademia etrusca dell'antichissima città di Cortona* (Essays of Academic Dissertations Publicly Read in the Noble Etruscan Academy of the very ancient city of Cortona).

The dissertations were elegantly illustrated with excellent engravings, and the topics covered were varied: they were not always about the Etruscans or Etruria. The monuments of Rome and Asia Minor are described by travellers and scholars, and some articles are eagerly devoted to questions of religious history.

Luigi Lanzi and the new Uffizi Gallery

The Florentine environment came to the fore again with the new arrangement of the Uffizi and the work of Luigi Lanzi (1732-1810), chosen as assistant to the director of the galleries, Giuseppe Pelli Bencivenni (1729-1808).

Lanzi had taught as a Jesuit at various colleges in Italy until the Society of Jesus was partially suppressed in 1767. Hired as an antiquarian assistant in the Florentine galleries, he was able to deepen his knowledge of archaeology, which earned him great fame, particularly for his studies of the Etruscans. The project of

The arcades of the Uffizi in a 19th century print.

reorganising the Gallery, which had just received a large quantity of new Etruscan material, brought Bencivenni's traditionalist approach into conflict with Lanzi's need for a modern and systematic presentation. This was in line with the wishes of Grand Duke Pietro Leopoldo, who wanted to open the museum to a wider public.

Working in Florence was also an opportunity for Lanzi to tackle the problem of language, which he approached with a clear and rational mind, proposing the application of the basic rules of philology. In the *Saggio di lingua etrusca*, the scholar recognised the affinity between the Etruscan and Greek alphabets, especially in their earliest stages, and arrived at a first overall decipherment that was essentially correct.[98] The essay was not only a linguistic treatise, but also a synthesis of Etruscan history and civilisation, making extensive use of epigraphic and archaeological sources.

The analysis was carried out without the bias and conditioning of antiquarianism, to which Lanzi was a complete stranger, preferring instead a focus on Greekness, which was quite prevalent in the culture of the time. It is no coincidence that he was responsible for the first clear position on the attribution to Greek artisans of numerous figured vases discovered in Italy, with his *De' vasi antichi dipinti vulgarmente chiamati etruschi* of 1806.[99]

With Lanzi, the study of Etruria emerged from antiquarianism and began to adopt scientific methods, albeit along a not always linear path, on the eve of the great boom in archaeological excavations in the nineteenth century.

The Etruscans at the Uffizi

The connection between the Uffizi and the Etruscans was an

98 Luigi Antonio Lanzi, *Saggio di lingua etrusca e di altre antichità d'Italia*, Paglierini, Roma 1789, pp. 588 e seg.

99 Luigi Antonio Lanzi, *De' vasi antichi dipinti volgarmente chiamati etruschi*, Fantosini, Firenze 1806, pp. 17 e seg.

important phase in the history of the famous Florentine museum, until it evolved into the image that we know today and that is known throughout the world.

When Francesco I founded the Uffizi, many Etruscan works and artefacts were destined for the collection and were stored in different parts of the gallery without any precise rationale. As we have seen, from the middle of the 18th century, with the Grand Duchy of Lorraines, the need for a scientific collocation became clearer and more necessary. Collections from other cities and museums, such as Volterra and Montepulciano, then arrived at the Uffizi. It was precisely after the arrival of this second collection (from the former Museo Bucelli) that the work of organising the multitude of ancient artefacts began, with the need to prove their authenticity and display them in the best possible way.

The artefacts from Montepulciano and elsewhere were therefore placed in the Loggetta del Buontalenti, on the upper floors of the Loggia dei Lanzi. The numerous urns, some of which can still be seen today in the National Archaeological Museum, were exhibited here. For the first time, the Etruscans were displayed in a small museum dedicated to them.

However, the "great bronzes" were exhibited together with other works in the Gabinetto dei Bronzi Antichi, and the Greek/Etruscan vases remained in the Gabinetto di Terra, until at least 1796. Then, under the direction of Tommaso Puccini, they were moved to a room very close to the Loggetta del Buontalenti, as part of a further reorganisation.[100]

Purchases from collectors and archaeological discoveries in Tuscany continued, and many finds arrived at the Uffizi in the first half of 19th century, thanks in particular to the work of Arcangelo Michele Migliarini, Royal Antiquary of the Uffizi (from 1835), who was in constant contact with the gallery and antiquarian circles. It was a very active period for the rediscovery

---

100 *Dagli Uffizi al MAF. Gli Etruschi e il loro ruolo significativo a Firenze nel corso del tempo*, in *Conosci Firenze*, www.conoscifirenze.it

of the Etruscans by antiquarians, also thanks to the success of an exhibition held in London in those years.[101]

However, the cultural and political interest in the Etruscans is a phenomenon that goes "in waves", experiencing moments of stasis, almost oblivion, followed by rediscovery. In the second half of the 18th century, the Etruscan artefacts in the Uffizi were much less remembered and collecting declined sharply.

In the middle of the century, many pieces were moved to a room at the beginning of the Vasari Corridor, thus in a location peripheral to the heart of the museum, however frequented by visitors. There was a need to create a new museum elsewhere, as the Uffizi was being characterised in other art-historical directions, from the Classical to the Renaissance.

In 1871 the National Archaeological Museum of Florence was founded. At first it was located in Via Faenza, and from 1880 it moved to Piazza Santissima Annunziata / Via della Colonna. A specific space was thus created for archaeological and, in particular, Etruscan works, in recognition of their importance. Over time, a large collection of Egyptian, Roman and other artefacts was added.

Today, the Archaeological Museum is still a point of reference for the understanding of Etruscan culture and, through its collection and activities, continues the commitment to Etruscan research that has always characterised the city of Florence. Many centuries ago, the city chose to be the guardian, protector and heir of the entire Etruscan world, absorbing its light and its secrets, for better or for worse.

The "Etruscan Renaissance", with its wonderful revival, with its glories and its shadows, can perhaps be said to have ended with the end of the Grand Duchy. But the curiosity about the "secrets" and the origins of the ancient Etruscans was not lost, much less today. They are still written about, both in essays and in

101 Ibidem.

social networks, often with great knowledge and sometimes with superficiality. Linguistic links with the Semitic world are claimed, but also Sardinian, Oriental, Asian or more or less Indo-European origins. The study of the Etruscan language, perhaps even more than of their art, still seems to be the place where the researcher finds the necessary confirmation to proceed with his hypotheses.

The debate does not seem to be dying out, and many people approach it *without knowing how many published texts and discussions have been held, how many scholars have proposed eccentric solutions or momentary political expediency ...* falling prey to the same fascination that we still feel today.

In this book we have tried, without pretending to be experts (which is not the author's role), to give an idea of the human breadth of this tradition, of how the inspiration of an Etruscan identity is one of the most vivid factors in our collective consciousness.

And how, if necessary, the chimera can emerge from the wilderness at any moment in Tuscan history.

Why in Tuscany?

The seeds of the Renaissance between society and landscape

by Lorenzo Pecchioni

According to Dionysius of Halicarnassus, the Rasna/ Rasenna people took their name from a mysterious eponymous hero, Rasenna,[102] one of the commanders of "an army of all the Etruscans"[103] to whom we may owe the political unification of the most important cities. This was part of a mission of conquest that lies at the mythical-historical foundation of the identity of this people. This information is often overlooked when we ask ourselves about the roots of the Etruscan civilisation, hypothesising oriental, Nordic or other origins, but first of all diverting our attention from the Tuscan-Lazio area, from the place of constitution of what became, in one way or another, a nation.

Even if we remain in the dark about the facts and myths of the actual unification, we should take into account the existence of such an undertaking, at least intuiting its symbolic significance in relation to the lands that were the object of it and in reflecting on the concept of Etruria in the most general sense. Although this may be a historiographical formalism or another operation of political communication,[104] Dionysius' mention of Rasenna allows us to deduce certain constitutive features of Etruscan national identity, or of what could be perceived as such in Roman times. The idea of a duke commanding an army; the existence of different ethnic

102 *Ant. Rom.* I, 30,3. Similarly, the Greek tradition tells of Tyrrhenians commanded by Tyrrhenus, but we do not know how far the two narratives may coincide.

103 The mention of Dionysius is interpreted as follows by L. Aigner Foresti in *Gli Etruschi e la loro autocoscienza*, in *Autocoscienza e rappresentazione dei popoli nell'antichità*, Vita e Pensiero, Milano 1992, p. 95.

104 It seems that Dionysius wanted to emphasise a direct link between the Romans and the Greeks, returning the Etruscans to an essentially autochthonous origin. At the same time, we cannot exclude the possibility that the military conquest to which the Etruscans (in a later period) may have alluded coincided with the legend of the Trojan War, and that they tended to place the origin of the idea of the Tyrrhenian union in this event.

matrices (Aborigines, Pelasgi, Arcadians...[105]); the necessary claim to territory, where this heterogeneity finds a coherent and political form. Conversely, other Etruscan-original characteristics, relating to specific aspects of society, may have been projected onto the figure of the leader, characterising him in meanings completely unknown to us.

Leaving aside the shaky historical data and coming to the aspects of the legendary-imaginary, the link between Rasenna and the Etruscan territory could be such that, hypothetically, he could be considered an emblematic figure for it, as in the case of other eponymous heroes. His military declination would suggest that the Etruscans, at the height of their achievements, felt proudly "Tuscan" and originally bound to their own land, in defiance of Lydia[106] and everything else. In this short essay, through a reflection on the territory, its image and the mythologies associated with it, I will try to present some elements for the intuition of a common denominator between ancient and modern Etruscans, starting from the existence of "dukes" or "condottieri" and beyond.

The unification of the territory

Although there was a moment of military concretisation - perhaps related, for modern Etruria, to the wars of Cosimo I - we can imagine the genesis of the ancient Etruscan federation as a slow process of mutual integration between the populations that arrived and spread across the territory. Cultural relations took place along pastoral and commercial routes, with constant exchanges between

105 *Ant. Rom.* I, 30 e seg.

106 Herodotus states their origin from this region (Histories, I,94). We do not know what precisely the Etruscans thought about their origins. Perhaps some of them included among their traditions that of coming from the East. This probably gained importance in the course of the Hellenistic influences (5th-4th centuries). Then Rasenna would have coincided with Rasus or Résos, a warrior in the Iliad who is said to have led a union of the Tyrrhenians in the Trojan conflict. On the analogy between these heroes see also Gabriele Morolli, *Vetus Etruria*, Allinea, Rome 1985 cf. G. Quispel, Gli Etruschi nel Vecchio Testamento, StEtr, Florence 1940, p. 419. On the imagery / vision of oriental origins I refer to *Il risveglio di Fufluns*, Press & Archeos, Florence 2017, p. 75 ff.

the ports of the Maremma and the hinterland, influencing various aspects of the Etruscan world. In a religious sense, for example, the Apennine cults were refined and adapted to Mediterranean mythologies. Habits and customs known from the interaction with different peoples found a new and original synthesis.

We can perhaps hypothesise that the transmission of ideas and the development of society in Tuscany, both in ancient and modern times, had a peculiar rhythm, largely influenced by the morphology of the territory. As it were, the texture of the landscape had already favoured the intuition of similarities and differences, suggesting the layout of settlements, the grid of roads and the geometry of fields, as well as the same predilection for those crops that were to become characteristic.

I believe it is important, albeit conceptually ethereal, the relationship between society and landscape, precisely because in it can be traced a primarily valid factor, then as now and in the Renaissance. Besides determining customs and traditions, this factor seems to correspond to a deeper existential disposition. The landscape, seen and experienced, postulates or encloses the possibility of identity development, and it is perhaps this possibility that Rasenna and her men appropriate, in the course of an emblematic myth-historical tale that we have almost completely lost; besides, as we shall see, other tales would have been produced from the same matrix.

Climate, crops, participation

Moderate average annual temperatures with a well-defined winter season; rainfall distributed throughout the year and prevailing in certain seasons; marked but not excessive night-night excursions: between the Arno and the Tiber, to the west of the Apennines, the ancient colonisers of Etruria found an ideal, temperate climate that favoured the attraction of ethnic groups from Europe and the Mediterranean, from the north and the east.

The most recent echoes of this extraordinariness resonate in rural traditions, which tell of triple rains in sunny Augusts, winters as cold as summers are hot, March winds that bring essences, ashen moons that encourage harvests, and a Faflon, the Etruscan Fufluns/ Dionysus who protects the harvests.[107] By crossing Sylvan vines with varieties from Magna Graecia, the Etruscan winegrowers found a considerable advantage in the Tuscan climate. Viticulture is perhaps the most representative synthesis of the "Etruscan fusion" (a sort of "blend" of peoples), because it was able to create and spread well-being, liveliness, inspiration, which were the foundations of a free and cosmopolitan world.

Of course, the great Rome did not exist at that time, but in the disputes between the inhabitants of Veio (or other Etruscan towns) and the Latin peoples, and in the conflicts that pitted the Etruscans, Celts and Romans against each other, we can see more than one analogy. In fact, the Etruscan federation was interrupted before the Tiber, beyond which the factor/denominator that had allowed and protected the unification further north was less sensitive: the landscape itself changed and other peoples shared the pastures.

The society that Cosimo and Rasenna left behind after their conquests was thus modelled on the essential concepts of climate and geography: balanced and therefore even democratic - certainly more so than in the case of other ancient peoples - it was even recognised as republican by Renaissance scholars. It is a world in which the individual enjoys a good deal of freedom of expression, in which traditional assumptions are reinterpreted with flair, in which there is a moderate degree of equality between ethnic groups, social classes and the sexes, and in which some of the work is assigned to outsiders (in crafts as well as military activities) who are welcomed with goodwill. Different energies seem to find a common circuit to express themselves.

---

107 Giovannangelo Camporeale, *Gli Etruschi. Storia e civiltà*, Utet, Torino 2005, p. 209.

Above all, however, it is possible to recognise the existence of an aristocracy that sought to establish itself through the display of wealth and beauty: through goldsmithing, patronage and even collecting. The Etruscan lords, like the collectors of Cosimi's Tuscany, were already connoisseurs of Greek vases (initially mistaken by archaeologists for genuine Etruscan vases[108]).

The Etruscan oligarchies undoubtedly had their own source of inspiration; they did not hesitate to expand and plough the sea, founding emporiums all over Italy, in the north, on the French coast, even with a treasury in Delphi (named after the city of Cere). To return to the parallel with the Renaissance, we know that in the 16th century the Tyrrhenian Sea was ploughed by ships as it had not been since antiquity. In addition to the mercantile activities carried out throughout Europe, we remember that the only Italian expedition to conquer lands in the New World belonged to the Medici.

In spite of these expansionist synergies, we note that the claim to possession of the territory still stopped within original Etruria, while elsewhere they tried to assert themselves by other means.

In these different temporal contexts, distant from each other but united by a spatiality that is also a breadth of vision - by an inspiration that urges the expression and preservation of one's own excellence - the work of masters flourishes; houses and mausoleums are enriched; the bodies of women, men and slaves are embellished; apparatuses for consumption and pleasure are created and earthly pleasures are celebrated with statues, ceramics, bronzes, paintings. In short, all this gives the impression that some essence of Renaissance flair was present long before the Renaissance itself.

It is as if this "seeds" had remained in a special diapause, ready to awaken when new elements and new circumstances could ensure its full manifestation: waiting for a sudden advance or shock of history.

---

108 The definitive attribution of most of the ceramic finds to Greek craftsmen is attributable to Luigi Lanzi, in *De' vasi antichi dipinti volgarmente chiamati etruschi*, 1806.

This passage would also have to do with the emergence of the Florence of the merchants and intellectuals, and the decisive element would be the presence of a new Porsenna/Rasenna, embodied first by Lorenzo and then, with striking relevance, by Cosimo I. Then the spirit of the lucumone or "Tagete" could re-emerge from the land, just as archaeological images reappear from the Tuscan subsoil.

Let us see where this seemingly vague and dreamy analogy can lead us.

The seed of the Renaissance in the landscape

We should speak of a seed rather than a gene, perhaps to avoid entering into the question of the genetic links between contemporary Tuscans and ancient Etruscans, a complex and somewhat controversial subject. In fact, it seems interesting to evaluate a kind of environmental inheritance, the reflection of individuals in a particular articulation between climate, territory and history, which becomes a metaphor through the image of the landscape.

In this case, the seed is to the gene what the landscape is to the territory, and to "prefer" the former means to look beyond the materially understood history and thus to turn to the myth and the instances it represents. Exceptional landscapes can inspire particular mental dispositions in any part of the world, and so it is in Etruria.

The morphology of the Etruscan environment was more or less the same from antiquity to modern times, evolving consistently until the partial abandonment of the countryside due to the economic and industrial boom. The original and already promiscuous landscape, in which man moved and of which he was an integral part, is closely linked to that painted by the artists of the Renaissance - from Paolo Uccello to Leonardo da Vinci - according to a series of variables that, beyond the filter of style, leave behind certain fundamental characterisations: moderation, elegance, alternation, depth, a kind of slight ambiguity...

Although in ancient times everything was wilder and there were fewer crops, roads and settlements, the morphological essence of the landscape is the same capable of attracting its spectator in modern times. For example, if we look at the roads of the Rasna, traced by the medieval routes and today's trekking routes, winding over the hills, curious and elegant: sometimes it seems as if all the places had to be connected at the expense of complicating the main route. The course of history has been sifted, slowed down and completed by the series of hills that "rhythmically protect" it. In short, in the very essence of the places there is the intention to unite and in this the capacity to poetize, to round off, to protect. We can find the same tension, as authoritative as italic, in the fictile statuary, in the goldsmithing, in the painting of the Rasna; as in the words of the Renaissance scholars who, in the Florentine vernacular, extolled an ideal Etruscan society.[109]

Already in ancient times, along the sides of the paths, scrubland opened up, later alternating with crops, the first rows of which were marked out and protected by hedges.

This plot would have developed in a context in which the hills, of similar heights and shapes, bounded by *lame*[110] and gullies, create secular units in which the various elements (human and natural) are manifested in the same quantity and with heterogeneous qualities. This creates a "harmonious message" capable of responding in a simple, clear and vivid way to the needs of the soul: to accommodate the sacred and to give meaning, a path to the everyday dimension.

In the need and the intention to participate in the landscape, in the encounter with history, in dealing with the vagaries of this territory and in taking advantage of them, we find typical developments that reinforce the analogy between circumstances distant in time. The landscape we are dealing with today, which

109 I wrote about this in *Il Quarto Chianti*, Press & Archeos, Firenze 2012, p. 36 e seg.

110 An ancient Latin word, also used in Italian, meaning a large puddle or small lake; sometimes a swamp. This word is very diffused in the toponomastic of Tuscany.

represents one of the most important Etruscan patrimonies, is that of the world-famous photographs: Chianti, Val d'Orcia, Maremma, Tuscia laziale and other sub-regions that are universally recognised for their ability to seduce with plastic aesthetic tension. The suggestion evoked by panoramas was undoubtedly already felt in ancient times, although the link with the earth was still energetically rooted and there was no landscape art capable of extracting and abstracting the viewer or spectator.

The vitality of the landscape

In the introduction to the *Carta del Chianti*, Paolo Baldeschi recognises that among the landscapes that most characterise the identity of the heart of Tuscany is the so-called "patchwork", i.e. the alternation in the hilly context of areas of vine cultivation, olive groves, small wooded areas and areas of settlement.[111] One of the rules of sustainability of this landscape is the balance between the erosion of the hilly soil and its reformation by processes of pedogenesis;[112] a phenomenon that has been refined over the centuries and that we can perhaps already see in antiquity, at least in places close to the main lucumonies. In fact, the continuity of vine and olive cultivation is one of the most important factors in the anthropisation of the Etruscan territory.

The "patchwork" is already clearly visible in some paintings of the 15th century and plays an interesting role in the works of Paolo Uccello, in particular in the Battaglia di San Romano, whose theme is the dualism between Florence and Siena, the very cornerstone of the unification of Renaissance Etruria. Beyond the combatants, the background imposes itself, leaving no room for the sky, with a tapestry of fields, clusters of trees and vineyards

111 Paolo Baldeschi in *La carta del Chianti*, edited by Fabio Lucchesi, Passigli, Bagno a Ripoli 2010, p. 7 ff. I dealt with these aspects in *Il Quarto Chianti*, Press & Archeos, Florence 2012, p. 13 ff.

112 Paolo Baldeschi, "La carta del Chianti", cit, p. 11.

Above, detail from Paolo Uccello's Battle of San Romano; below, frescoes from Etruscan tombs (5th–4th century BC).

arching over small hills.[113]

The landscape beyond the battle seems to present itself not as an object of contention, but as a sounding board and a celebration. The historical event becomes a symbolic theme and takes on an existential significance in terms of the unification of Tuscan souls. Of all those who, initially "spectators" of the landscape, had intentions towards it and descended into the territory to identify and merge with it. Meanwhile, we imagine the ancient Etruscans, now invisible and definitively united to their land, dancing eternally among the hedges as they appear in the funerary frescoes; but in Paolo's painting their spirit seems to penetrate the small figures of archers and duellists lost in the rustic background ... in an evocative parallelism.

In this way, unity may be manifested through the instrument of

113 I refer in particular to the episode of the *Unseating of Bernardino della Ciarda*, preserved in the Uffizi (1438).

war, but this does not seem - when we look at certain paintings or read certain celebratory texts - to be an unquestionable value, as it is in other cultures and often in the neighbouring Roman world. Instead, it is the battlefield itself, or the struggle that becomes a shape in the landscape, that suggests other strategic possibilities, perhaps in fidelity to an idea of participation in the harmonious solutions offered by nature. And in the implicit conviction that good governance, based on harmonious balances, is fruitful and prosperous.

Looking at Ambrogio Lorenzetti's famous Sienese fresco, the *Allegory of Good Government*, and those rural landscapes in which "patchworks" appear, we are reminded of the words of the Chancellor Leonardo Bruni, who praised Etruria as the cradle of republican civilisation[114]. And we get the impression that it is precisely by longing for the landscape, by descending into it with inspiration and reason, that ancient and modern people have come to value similar ideals.

The "genius" of the landscape seems to suggest to us that neither Etruscans nor Medici lucumoni, no duke from these lands could have conquered all of Italy with iron and fire: warlike conquest is not in the seed of Tuscany, even if the soul of the landscape may suggest its strategic urgency and clearly its propagandistic instrumentalisation. There is no doubt that Lorenzo and Cosimo needed, above all, battles to depict.

Even the lost myth of Rasenna could be an ancestral manifestation of this need.

The landscape that 'speaks' through legend

The italian word *paesaggio*, derived from the French *paysage* (a concept closely linked to artistic experience), refers above all to a part of the territory as it appears to the observer. And the

114 *Leonardo Bruni Historiarum fiorentini populi libri XII*, started in 1414. Ed. S. L. Zetzneri, 1610, p. 3.

viewer/spectator must perhaps be the real protagonist of a study of landscape itself. The study of landscape can lead away from the material emergence, because it is always and in any case a mood, a mental and sometimes nostalgic image of the face of the earth, a fundamental statement of the human problematic.[115] In other words, it seems that a study of landscape cannot be exempt from the projection of archetypes that come alive in the collectivity and anticipate new possibilities of action in the wake of atavistic experiences. In our case, this collectivity and this "spectator" are timelessly Etruscan.

Perhaps it was when Renaissance scholars rediscovered the essentially pagan basis of rural culture that a conscious contact with this landscape emerged. In the countryside, the pagus (villages) had held out for centuries with their inexhaustible traditions and customs. Then the *genius loci* awoke from centuries of torpor and the woods were filled with numerous mediators: nymphs, heroes, wild kings, demons, adapted to the context of a 'golden age'.

The primordial figures of the origins of peoples and the foundations of cities were revived or invented, distilled from the chaos of necessity and projected into an imaginary world inspired, sometimes by a certain drunkenness; and perhaps it was the love of wine, so strongly felt in Etruria, that preserved and magnified this earthly community and made the view of the landscape more fertile.[116]

In addition to the many sublime artistic representations, we find remarkable examples of mythical narrative in early Florentine historiography and beyond. Fascinating legends about Etruscan Fiesole, its founding by Attalante and Elettra, and many minor characters (who would find a full narrative dimension in Boccaccio's *Ninfale fiesolano*), were circulated and collected in Florence.

Through the adventures of Affrico and Mensola (both names

115 *Il Quarto Chianti*, Press & Archeos, Firenze 2012 p. 15.

116 I explored the relationship between wine inebriation and landscape in *Il risveglio di Fufluns*, Press & Archeos, Florence 2017.

of local streams) in their relationship with Diana and Attalante, King of Fiesole, the essence of the landscape seems to come alive. We are talking about the Fiesole hills, clearly visible from Florence, crossed by "patchworks". There, in their villas, the lords drank to earthly pleasures and measured the distance between reality and myth. Among the legends is the figure of Fiorino, a Florentine hero of the same name, about whom Malispini wrote as early as the 13th century.1[117] It is said that Caesar wanted this condottiere to lead the Roman soldiers besieging Fiesole. However, the Fiesolians managed to assassinate him in a night ambush. As Fiorino's blood was spread on the ground near the Arno, the lilies that bloomed there took on a red colour.

The pre-Synectic hilly landscape, from whose forests the first seeds of a civilised society emerged thanks to the efforts of kings, heroes and condottieri, finds its paradigm in the legends of the very ancient history ("*storia antichissima*") of Lazio. Just as Alba Longa (the mythical kingdom from which Romulus and Remus came) introduces the history of Rome, so Fiesole must introduce the greatness of Florence. The analogies are numerous and are rooted in the visual nature of the origins of the place names: Alba, destined to produce the civilisation of popes and emperors, is distinguished in the landscape by the whitish colour of its mountain,[118] while Fiesole, destined to identify Florentine civilisation, is distinguished by its solitude (fiat sola); but these are symbolic conditions of a distinction in and from the territory and of a new view of it.

In fact, the legends of the founding of Rome, told by Plutarch, Titus Livy, Dionysius and others, should be considered as the starting point for the fantasies of the scholars of the 14th century and the Renaissance, even if they were oriented towards other

117 Ricordano Malispini, *Storia fiorentina*, Multigrafica, Roma 1976, pp. 9-10.

118 The etymology of Alba has produced extensive speculation. On this subject, see already Giovanni Antonio Riccy, *Memorie storiche dell' antichissima città di Alba-Longa e dell' Albano moderno*, Zempel, Roma 1787, pp. 20-21.

places. As in the case of the Fiesole Etruscans, the Roman landscape is a succession of hills, woods and springs, and we see the uncertain existences of Saturn, Pico, Faunus and Latino. We witness their attempts to organise shepherds and savages, the aborigines mentioned by Dionysius, who may correspond to the Etruscans themselves. Faunus and Pico prophesy the future from the depths of the woods, giving meaning to the possibilities expressed by the landscape, and are the inhabitants of the mountains, masters of a paradoxical kingdom, since "it is not only devoid of urban centres, but also of rural centres".[119] It is the image of a state of human evolution: the landscape, offering itself as an existential metaphor, incubates equally "imaginary" characters, sometimes eponymous, but still only sketched out. They initiate a process of mutual integration between chronological society and timeless values.

Until the appearance of Romulus, "the state of civilisation [is] never fully achieved",[120] as if a compromise with the territory - an identity with its naturalistic archetypes - is struggling to come to an end. Then, with a new 'generation' of heroes, it seems to be the individual who, in the wake of necessity but inspired by the landscape, aspires, conquers and renames places. The whole anthropic complex is thus introduced into the course of history.

An example of this is the story of the leader of the city of Vulci, Aulus Vibenna, his brother Celius and their confidant Macstarna (later king of Rome under the name of Servius Tullius). Here, among other things, we see the idea of the link between the hero and the hill, in this case the Caelian (Monte Celio, actually conquered by the Etruscans in the 6th century BC).

As in this very rare example of a truly Etruscan historical tradition, perhaps Rasenna was also, in a mythical time, a daring leader and a king able to distinguish himself from the previous "wild kings". He would be one of those heroes whose blood ties to

119 Augusto Fraschetti, *Romolo il fondatore*, Laterza, Roma – Bari 2002, p. 18.

120 *Ibid.*, p. 14 e seg.

the land still boil over. But who, by adjusting the 'genius loci', can become emblems of the landscape that inspires and guides them. We are thus witnessing a migration from a point of identity (with the territory) to a point of view (on the landscape), from which it is possible to yearn for a humanitarian and social conquest, an overcoming of the original materiality. Actual contact with this idea, which is mysteriously linked to the laws of nature, often means going beyond one's human limits and shedding one's blood. Remus dies on the map/plot of the new city; Aule and Macstarna are the protagonists of a disturbing series of murders;[121] Fiorino's lilies turn red after his murder; a similar solution, related to martyrdom, becomes crucial in early Christianity.

In fact, between Rome and Fiesole, that is to say in the whole of Etruria itself, legends about deities who populate the landscape and heroes who act on its fabric of signifiers, multiplied during the Renaissance. These heroes staged, in their very names, the birth of the city and the first steps towards its settlement.

Think of the myths about the origins of Cortona, in which Corito is the protagonist, the son of that Dardano who, in Tuscany, is said to have been fathered by Jupiter and Electra.[122] There are also the stories of the mythical Viterbo of Annio or, among the legends and places in the background, that of Lucolena «al tosco lito» ("to the Tuscan montain"), about which Michele di Lando writes in the 14th century. Here the name of a place is deconstructed until another mythical story is projected, in which the forest takes on a personal form, that of Lena. The examples of stories are numerous and often have no precedent in ancient sources: they are inventions inspired by a new relationship with the landscape, which, having finally overcome the "dark" centuries, is rediscovered in all its emotional glory.

121 The sequence, depicted in the tomb of François at Vulci (4th century BC), represents the liberation of Caile by Macstarna, followed by other murders in an anti-Roman context.

122 G. Spini, E. Pecchioni, *Figli di Enea*, Press & Archeos, Firenze 2014, p. 77 e seg.

And still today...

But this anthropomorphic projection of the image of the territory seems to be a never-ending possibility, part of every phase of the reintegration of the past, and it persists in our "Etruscan-tourist" age, linked to new forms of wealth and consumerist tensions. Examples abound in advertising and marketing, but also in art and communication in general. I am thinking of the numerous installations of contemporary art in many parts of Tuscany. I am also quoting a text in an advertising brochure about Chianti:

(...) *From the happy union of "fusis" and "sofos", from their "love" was born a kind of divinity: the nymph of Chianti, the soul of these lands. She has the hair of blackberries and vines, the breath of the wind, the eyes of the stream, the blood of the wine, the soft body of the hills, the smile of the sun, the proud character of the castles and the tenderness of the badias, the spirit of rural concreteness and mystic asceticism, the age of millennia and the bearing of youthful elegance. / And it is capable of bizarre magic: it astonishes when it shows itself, fascinates when it tells, welcomes when it receives, inflames when it desires, and reveals itself mysteriously in its fulfilment only to those who have the patience and the spirit to penetrate its origin. This is the encounter between thought and nature.*[123]

With these words, Carlo Cambi has well illustrated the emotional characteristics of Chianti, giving us an example of how, even today, the reference to myth can merge with the intuition of the landscape. But the phenomenon is clearly much more widespread and can affect many places in Etruria and Italy.

The 'macchia tuscanica' seems to have become, since the Renaissance and beyond, a measured and positive case of a 'nearby forest'. The landscape was thus understood "not so much in terms

123 Carlo Cambi, da *Chianti/Terre di Siena*, APT Siena.

of the contours of the exploited land, but as a unified world with its surprises, its fears (...) its secret powers of fertility".[124] At the same time, forest and shadow, field and soul, land and ego harmonise with each other. The sylvan and rural nature, the king of the forest or the witch-fairy, are not banished to the unreachable mountain or the inaccessible abyss, but a path is always open to achieve an oracular contact, sometimes even in ironical way.

That is why I do not think it is enough to think of the hero's detachment (virile but complex, dramatic but fruitful...) from the bonds of identity with the land (a phenomenon that seems to go hand in hand with the emergence of those harmonious values already present in the image of the land and now destined to unite the articulations of society). The bond seems to lose its energy if man and his world are not able to look backwards and forwards, to synthesise new solutions or, if necessary, to reactivate the sacred tradition that makes it possible to reunite with the land.

This interweaving of possibilities is maintained, in the metaphor of the Etruscan landscape, by a certain alternation and balance. Thus, also through the structuring of the patchwork: the lucidity of a union that respects the diversity of its constituent elements.

The observations we have made seem to confirm the need for an existential union with the landscape and, through this, a possible renewal of one's world. A renewal that can also be, in many ways, a rebirth (a *reinassance*). And which can convey the relationship between identity and inspiration, between gene and "genius", highlighting the analogy between ancient and modern tensions, Etruscan and otherwise.

On the other hand, if the landscape loses its sense of depth, is reduced to a mere object of imaginary exploitation, even to an

---

124 G. Dumézil, *La religion romaine archaique*, Parigi 1974, p. 350 quote in A. Fraschetti, "Romolo...", cit., p. 21.

alibi for avoiding a real questioning of the stereotypes of one's own society ... then the *eponymous hero* disappears definitively. And there is no more rebirth or, in this case, no more Etruria.

Bibliography

(Books edited since the 18th century cited in the text)

AA. VV., *Dizionario Biografico degli Italiani*, Istituto dell'Enciclopedia Italiana, Roma 1979

Aigner Foresti Luciana, *Gli Etruschi e la loro autocoscienza*, in *Autocoscienza e rappresentazione dei popoli nell'antichità*, Vita e Pensiero, Milano 1992

Ammirato Scipione, *Istoria Fiorentina*, Marchini & Becherini, Firenze 1824

Andrieux Maurice, *I Medici*, Dall'Oglio, Milano 1978

Bargellini Piero, *I Medici*, Bonechi, Firenze 1980

Ibid. La Splendida Storia di Firenze, Vallecchi 1964

Bargellini P., Guarnieri E., *Le strade di Firenze*, Bonechi, Firenze 1977

Bartoloni G., Bocci Pacini P., *The importance of Etruscan antiquity in the Tuscan Renaissance*, in *The rediscovery of antiquity: the role of the artist*, Acta Hyperborea 10, 2003

Ibid. La divulgazione di scoperte di antichità etrusche a Firenze da Lorenzo a Cosimo, in *Archeologia Classica* vol. 56, L'Herma di Bretschneider, 2005

Bloch Raymond, *Gli Etruschi*, Il Saggiatore, Milano 1977

Bernardini Marzolla Piero, *L'Etrusco una lingua ritrovata*, Mondadori, Milano 1984

Bonciani Mauro, *Le Grandi battaglie Toscane*, Le Lettere, Firenze 2010

Borghini Vincenzo, *Dell'Origine della città di Firenze*, in *Discorsi di Monsignor Don Vincenzo Borghini*, Viviani, Firenze 1755

Burke Peter, *Il Rinascimento europeo*, Gius. Laterza & Figli, Roma-Bari 1998

Camporeale Giovannangelo, *Gli Etruschi, storia e civiltà*, UTET, Torino 2005

Cantini Lorenzo, *Vita di Cosimo de' Medici primo granduca di Toscana*, Firenze 1805

Cellini Benvenuto, *Vita di Sé Medesimo*, Cocchi, 1728

Cipriani Giovanni, *Il mito etrusco nel rinascimento fiorentino*, Olschki, Firenze 1980

Colivicchi Fabio, *L'antiquaria etrusca*, in *Gli Etruschi* a cura di Mario Torelli, Bompiani, Milano 2000

CRISTOFANI MAURO, *Il mito etrusco in Europa fra XVI e XVIII secolo* in *Gli Etruschi e l'Europa*, Fabbri Editori, Milano 1992

DEECKE WILHELM, *Etruskische Forschungen*, Stoccarda 1875-1880

ECO, UMBERTO, *Sulle spalle dei giganti*, La Nave di Teseo, Milano 2017

FERRINI ANTONIO, *Compendio di Storia della Toscana*, Sansone Coen, Firenze 1840

FRASCHETTI AUGUSTO, *Romolo il fondatore*, Laterza, Roma – Bari 2002

FUBINI RICCARDO, *Annio da Viterbo nella tradizione erudita toscana* in *Storiografia dell'Umanesimo in Italia da Leonardo Bruni ad Annio da Viterbo*, Storia e Letteratura, Roma 2004

GIGLI GIROLAMO, *Del Collegio petroniano delle balie latine e del solenne suo aprimento in quest'anno 1719*, Francesco Quinza, Siena 1719

GARIN EUGENIO, *Prosatori Latini del Quattrocento in La Letteratura Italiana. Storia e Testi*, Ricciardi, Napoli/Milano 1952.

GIULIANO ANTONIO (a cura di), *G. B. Piranesi - Della magnificenza ed architettura de' romani*, Il Polifilo, Milano 1993

GUARNIERI GIUSEPPE GINO, *L'ultima impresa coloniale di Ferdinando I dei Medici. La spedizione R. Thornton al Rio Amazonas, all'Orenoco, all'isola Trinidad, Livorno*, Stab. Tipografico Meucci, Firenze 1910.

HALE JOHN RIGBY, *Firenze e i Medici*, Mursia, Milano 1980

KELLER WERNER, *La Civiltà Etrusca*, Garzanti, Milano 1971

H.G. KOENIGSBERGER, G.L. MOSSE, G.Q. BOWLER, *L'Europa del Cinquecento*, Gius. Laterza & Figli, Roma-Bari 1990

LAPINI AGOSTINO, *Diario fiorentino, dal 252 al 1596*, Sansoni, Firenze 1900

LANZA ANTONIO (a cura di), *Giovanni Gherardi - Il Paradiso degli Alberti*, Sa- lerno ed., Roma 1975

LANZI, LUIGI ANTONIO, *Saggio di ligua etrusca e di altre antichità d'Italia*, Paglierini, Roma 1789

Ibid., *De' vasi antichi dipinti volgarmente chiamati etruschi*, Fantosini, Firenze 1806

LUCCHESI FABIO (a cura di), *La carta del Chianti*, Passigli, Bagno a Ripoli, 2010

MALISPINI RICORDANO, *Storia fiorentina*, Multigrafica, Roma 1976

MANCINI NICCOLÒ, *Orazioni e discorsi storici sopra l'antica città di Fiesole*, Arnaldo Forni, Firenze 1729

MONTAIGNE, MICHEL DE, *Viaggio in Italia*, BUR Milano 2003

MOROLLI GABRIELE, *Vetus Etruria-il mito degli Etruschi nella letteratura architettonica nell'arte e nella cultura da Vitruvio a Winckelmann*, Alinea, Firenze 1985

Museo Archeologico Nazionale di Firenze – *Minerva, Chimera, Arringatore*, schede descrittive

Pecchioni Enio, *La storia di Fiesole*, SP44, Firenze 1979

Ibid. Etruschi, il vincolo dell'unità sacrale, Press & Archeos, Firenze 2012.

Pianu Giampiero, *Gli Etruschi cinque miti da sfatare*, Armando Curcio Editore, 1985

Piranesi Giovan Battista, *Diverse maniere d'adornare i cammini ed ogni altra parte degli edifizi desunte dall'architettura Egizia, Etrusca e Greca con un Ragionamento Apologetico in defesa dell' architettura Egizia, e Toscana*, Parigi 1836

Riccy Giovanni Antonio, *Memorie storiche dell'antichissima citta di Alba-Longa e dell' Albano moderno*, Zempel, Roma 1787

Romagnoli Ugo, *I Medici-profili e vicende*, Cappelli, Bologna 1939

Salviati Leonardo, *Orazione III, In lode della fiorentina lingua e dei Fiorentini autori indiretta allo Ill. ed Ecc. Signor Don Francesco de' Medici*, 1564, edita in *Orazioni del cavaliere Lionardo Salviati*, Società tipografica de' Classici Italiani, Milano 1810

Scarpellini Margherita, Refice Paola, Secondino Gatta, *Andrea Sansovino, profeta in patria*, Icona, Arezzo 2016

Segni Bernardo, *Storie fiorentine di Messer Bernardo Segni*, Raimondo Mertz, Augusta 1723

Signorelli Mario, *Le vie segrete degli Etruschi*, Sugar Editore, Milano 1973

Spini Giorgio, *Cosimo de' Medici e l'indipendenza del principato mediceo*, Firenze 1945

Spini G., Pecchioni E., *Figli di Enea*, Press & Archeos, Firenze 2014

Valtieri, Simonetta, *Il «revival» etrusco nel Rinascimento toscano*, in *L'Architettura*, XVII, Etas Kompass, Milano 1971

Vannucci Marcello, *I Medici*, Roma 1987

Vasari Giorgio, *Le Opere*, con annotazioni e commenti di G. Milanesi, Sansoni, Firenze 1906

Ibid. Le Vite dei più eccellenti pittori scultori ed architetti, Firenze 1878

Verga Marcello, *Dicembre 1569: la concessione del titolo granducale ai Medici* in *Portale Storia di Firenze, Firenze* 2012 (http://www.storidifirenze.org/)

Villani Giovanni, *Nuova Cronica*, Fondazione Pietro Bembo/Ugo Guanda Editore, Parma 1990

Weege Fritz, *Etruskische malerei*, Halle 1921

Young, George Frederick, *I Medici*, Salani, Firenze 1987

Content

Addendum

Florence
2023

www.ingramcontent.com/pod-product-compliance
Lightning Source LLC
LaVergne TN
LVHW041104150826
845673LV00007B/1919

* 9 7 9 1 2 8 2 1 3 4 0 0 2 *